HOW FISH WORK

DR. TOM SHOLSETH

Frank **A**mato
PORTLAND

All inquiries should be addressed to:
Frank Amato Publications, Inc.
P.O. Box 82112 • Portland, Oregon 97282
503-653-8108
www.amatobooks.com

Book Design: Amy Tomlinson
Cover photo by Scott Ripley
All other photos by Tom Sholseth, unless otherwise noted

Softbound ISBN: 1-57188-239-1
Softbound UPC: 0-66066-00493-2

Printed in Hong Kong
1 3 5 7 9 10 8 6 4 2

Table of Contents

Dedication

Tom Sholseth, DVM, MPVM

This book is dedicated to my lovely wife Janice. Thank you for your "you should just finish your book" support and for going fishing with me even though you aren't really into it. Thank you for believing in me, loving all the creatures, and a special thank you for loving the way I love nature.

Janice Sholseth

Acknowledgements

Special acknowledgement goes to Dan Barden, a wonderful novelist, friend and professor. I'm indebted to Seth Norman for his encouragement with this book and to our friend Richard Anderson for letting a fish doctor write for his magazine. I would also like to thank the Amato family for giving guys like me a chance to express themselves.

Thanks to all the science folks along the way, my professors, pals at the fish lab, patients, clients and colleagues. Thanks Steve Spellman, Jim Kittell, Lee Selmes, Mike St. John Smith, Joel and especially Beluga Larry (and Judy).

I'd also like to acknowledge the Possibility People. . . Werner, Tami, Anurag, David Miles, Ellen, Mags, MB, and all my friends that have joined me in the conversational Forum for possibility.

I'm forever deeply indebted to Dr. Lou Smith: Man, was I lucky you showed up.

Last but not least, I'd like to thank my mother, Frances Smith. This all started with you pointing to science and Nature with that toad in the carport in Dallas.

In Memory

MR. MULLIGAN:

Fish retriever extraordinaire

"Where's my brown dog,

where's my hound?

He loved my truck, he hung around.

They've all gone to Mexico. . ."

Willie Nelson, "Half-Nelson"

Introduction

"The male has more teeth than the female in mankind, and sheep and goats, and swine. This has not been observed in other animals. Those persons which have the greatest number of teeth are the longest lived; those which have them widely separated, smaller, and more scattered, are generally more short lived."

Aristotle (384-322 BCE), Greek philosopher.
History of Animals.

10 p.m., June 21, 2000 (Summer Solstice): Taking a moment for a quick photo, the author releases this estuarine Cook Inlet chinook so it can resume its upstream migration.

This book didn't turn out the way I thought it would. Originally, I had notions of writing the definitive fish science book for anglers.

I didn't. It isn't.

I also thought that a love of angling and a veterinary medical degree was enough to prepare me for the effort.

I was wrong.

So I augmented my education as a veterinarian with a specialty in fish medicine. Even as I did so, however, I fully expected it would be relatively simple to compile of the scientific information pertinent to angling and relate this to established fishing practice.

You may have guessed. I soon found out that much of our fishing gospel—that which is taken on faith by our angling community—has no basis in science at all (or, for that matter, even in logic).

It's bunk, to put it bluntly. But at the same time as I was exploring and attempting to understand aspects of our collective ignorance, including my own, I was discovering a body of knowledge for which a wise angler would eagerly trade a favorite rod. Debunking on one hand, proposing on the other. . . consider these twin efforts the pylons supporting a bridge over a substantial gap in our understanding.

For example:

A primary assumption of most anglers is that fish see the world the way we do. If a fly it looks good to us, or appeals to what we imagine fish sensibility might be, it's admired. It's also fished, and will sometimes work, so gets talked about, becomes the subject of articles, which are reprinted, complied in books, eventually nominalized, "Anglers IV: Chapter Three: Verse Seven."

Do you doubt it's that simple, even silly?

Aristotle revealed to the world that women had fewer teeth than men did. His discovery became dental dogma, an article of faith that survived more than a thousand years.

It was never true, of course; yet even with hard as enamel evidence to the contrary right under the nose of a hundred generations; Ari's error lived on as "fact." To repudiate it was bicuspid blasphemy.

This book counts teeth. It doesn't split hairs—we aren't always out-of-line; but it will offer a variety of alternate explanations of how fish work. It's my attempt to consider aspects of angling from the perspective of a fish, not from an underwater human perspective, because fish don't see the world the way we do. Fish have their own "perceptual world," a distinct "Merkvelt," as described by Dutch ethologist (animal behaviorist) Nikolass Tinbergen. This book tries to interpret that, and to translate the exigencies of their lives into the Merkvelt of anglers—offering in that attempt both conceptual and utilitarian information gleaned from research.

To what end?

When we start to understand the way fish view their world and see what "motivates" them, we begin to pick up trends. These trends are the footprints of principles. Once we understand the principles we can use them to our advantage in a variety of circumstances, instead of fishing to dogma. Angling becomes much more manageable when we start to "think" like fish.

Each angler brings with them their own unique understanding of his or her pastime and quarry. Some are technical experts in areas that intersect with angling and some have angling expertise specific only to their love of fishing. Hopefully this book has a little for everyone, expert and beginner.

I attempted to design this book so it can be read the way I read, a little at a time. Sometimes I'll only spend 5 minutes or if I read before I go to sleep at night, I'll take about 10 minutes. Each chapter and sidebar are self-contained, meaning they can be mostly understood by themselves without building on much prior information. In order to do this there's a certain amount of repetition of key principles in the sidebars that was presented in the body of the chapter. The first three chapters are pretty basic, the middle chapters seem more interesting to me and the last two should probably be read first if you're ready to commit to being a scientific angler.

One last note: I've addressed herein just a few of many topics anglers would find of interest in the large body of scientific knowledge already extant. More information is generated each hour, in laboratories around the world. The topics I included were just a few of those that struck me as particularly illuminating. I figured if they got me going they might interest other devotees.

Time will tell.

What is scientific angling?

"The joy of discovery is certainly the liveliest that the mind of man can ever feel."
Claude Bernard (1813-78) French physiologist.

What does the word "science" mean to you? When I think about my first encounter with science, I remember a disturbing conversation I had with my fourth grade teacher. At the time school wasn't too thrilling and the fourth grade wasn't showing much promise either. I didn't like reading much, except for a couple of books that were among that year's Christmas presents.

I loved those books. They were hardcover, with colorful pictures, about a half an inch thick, perfect for a nine-year-old. With them, insects, rocks, fish, mammals and oceans came alive. I inspected those books—my Dead Sea scrolls—repeatedly, just to make sure I hadn't missed some odd creature or strange truth that lurked undiscovered beyond the plowed cotton fields circumscribing my Texas childhood.

One day our fourth grade teacher introduced the North American phenomenon of grammar school known as "show and tell." We were instructed to give a talk on a topic we held dear and be prepared to display some representation of it in class the next day. My science books, of course!

When it was my turn at the fourth grade improv. I masterfully relayed the way these books made sense of what I saw in my backyard—and the promise of what lay beyond. Well, that's how I remember it; most likely, I just pointed a few times and talked about the frog and fish pictures.

After the presentation, our teacher (who I now refer to as the Bride of Mephistopheles) made some disparaging comment about my prize literary possessions: they were, she told me, more appropriate for lowly third graders. And I, she said, should grow up.

Now, it's quite possible that my memory has skewed this a bit during the last 40 years, but the incident left me with a deep shame of my love for science. Somehow, I hadn't gotten it right. From that point on, the word "science" became charged with extra significance for me.

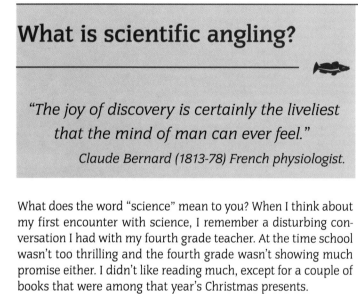

Documentation of early-childhood development.

I know. . . "Get over it." Point well taken, thanks, but the reason I recount this childhood trauma is to illustrate how we develop unique relationships to the word "science" (a malady related to "math anxiety"). To some, it comes to represent a discipline that's cold, impersonal and harsh. Others equate science with technology; the only solution to the world's ills. But just about everyone thinks it's interesting only to bookworms and nerds, i.e. the pocket-protector crowd.

OK, maybe. . . but then again maybe not.
We're all anglers here. What if it's really a scientific perspective that we've been looking for when we go fishing?

Webster's dictionary defines science as "systematic knowledge of the physical or material world gained through observation and experimentation." To me, this describes the angling modus operandi. If you replace the words "physical" and "knowledge" with "fish" and "angling" and you've defined the mantra of most avid anglers I know.

That is the main contention of this book: anglers are scientists. In their own way, fishers observe and experiment with systematic methods of capturing their species of interest.

We seek the true nature of things pertaining to fish. We understand "fish-truth" through observation and testing and to the degree we succeed, we catch fish. (The truth may set us free, but all fish are not so lucky.)

I think scientific anglers enjoy fishing more. Marrying science to angling doesn't diminish the "experience"; on the contrary, it enhances it. Human beings are inquisitive by nature. We love to figure things out. And really, if catching fish were too easy, we'd get bored, if too hard, we wouldn't do it.

There are lots of applications of scientific principles in angling. Take efficiency for example. Imagine you're catching fish with an Elk Hair Caddis. If it's working well you won't switch to another type of fly, unless you're a masochist. (Please excuse the redundancy with fly-fishing and masochism.)

If it works, don't fix it.

That said, there's still a lot of inefficiency in our angling habits. We expend a lot of effort doing things that don't work—and can't, given fish-reality. In a pinch we often appeal to Merlin and his magic fly, rather than to Carl Sagan and his method of observation.

I think this predilection fosters our lack of public credibility. We'll believe just about anything and everyone knows it. Not that there isn't a mutual conspiracy going on, our gullibility is vital to the angling industry. It sells "Big Bubba's Bass Busters."

Why haven't there been efforts to eliminate all the hype around fishing?

If all anglers used scientific principles and only did what worked there'd be a lot less gear on the market. Instead of spending resources marketing superfluous products—tackle that hooks anglers—the industry would have do legitimate clinical trials to determine what really works.

Until that happens, it's up to us to figure out what's efficient and effective. Applying the scientific method is a good way to start.

Science Methodology

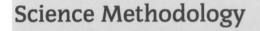

"The scientific method," Thomas Henry Huxley once wrote,
"is nothing but the normal working of the human mind."
That is to say, when the mind is working; that is to say further, when it is engaged in correcting its mistakes.
Taking this point of view, we may conclude that science is not physics, biology, or chemistry—is not even a "subject"—but a moral imperative drawn from a larger narrative whose purpose is to give perspective, balance, and humility to learning.

Neil Postman, The End of Education, Alfred A. Knopf, New York, 1995, p 68.

Have you ever been in a verbal sparring match with someone, and you just knew you were right, but because you couldn't communicate your point very well, you wound up looking stupid?

I have.

This happens a lot in the angling microcosm. The best talker wins. It has little to do with the facts, mostly debating technique. Ultimately, the truth will stand the test of time. But how do we tell what's the truth?

Human beings (anglers included) become very attached to their beliefs. It's understandable given a lack of a better explanation of what we observe, we hold on to the ones we've got. But a problem rests in the way our beliefs are formed. A good example of a belief attachment was western civilization's understanding of a person's identity.

It wasn't that long ago that people thought the unique center or "soul" of a human being resided in the organ called the heart. Sayings like "she has a lot of heart" and "have a heart" reflect this sentiment.

This theory had some evidence. Every time someone had his or her heart irreparably damaged, he would die and, sure enough, he assumed room temperature just like every other dead guy. And yes, if animals lost their heart, they died too! Pretty convincing argument really. You can see how easy it was to attribute special qualities to that organ.

The theory took a beating over time. But it wasn't until surgeons started performing heart surgery that we "proved" it wrong: give Zak a couple of pig valves and a transplant and you had your evidence. His new heart didn't carry the personality of the donor (a very nice motorcycle enthusiast) because Zak was the same old SOB.

There goes your "heart equals the center of being" theory.

So what does this have to do with fishing? Well, it's just possible that we as anglers have some beliefs that are a little outdated and could use some testing. This is where the scientific discipline of testing theories contributes to angling.

Can an angler do real scientific research on his or her own?

I think so and this book is an introduction to doing just that. Angler—meet science. Science—shake hands with angler.

Develop and test your angling theory: following your heart.

The scientific method is based on observation and testing. First, you observe something in nature, as in our previous hypothesis: humans and/or animals that lose their hearts are never the same. Next you develop a simple theory to explain your observations.

Medieval man's theory associated a "personality" or "soul" to a single pumping organ. Imagine yourself as a scientifically inclined medieval person, making predictions based on this theory. According to your hypothesis, if your buddy (Izaak) loses his heart, he, as a distinct individual would cease to exist. Armed with this expectation, you now carefully observe what happens while you test your theory.

Gutted like a carp, Izaak proves no exception to the past results. Saddened by the loss, yet uplifted by the acquisition of new information (and his rod), you conclude your theory correct: people need a heart to have a distinct personality or being. Somewhat smug in your abilities as an observer of nature, you proceed to expound ad-nauseum to all your buddies at the local tackle shop. Now they all know the facts.

These particular facts had a shelf life of about 300 years, until someone eventually figured out a way to switch a damaged heart for a low-mileage model. Still testing your theory, you (by now you're getting really old) read in the newspaper how a fly purist received the heart of a worm fisherman yet remained a feather-and-fur devotee.

Now, what do you do?

According to the scientific method, you modify your theory in light of new results. Apparently the personality doesn't reside in the heart. (Bummer Izaak.) Your new hypothesis might be "personality, individuality or distinct being may not reside in the heart, but you have to have a heart to live." Now you go back to testing your theory and making more observations in the world.

This might seem like a step back, but it's not. You learned something. You didn't figure out what caused personality, but you did discover that it isn't permanently linked to a specific heart. Although that's a negative informational fact, it's a beginning.

You and I, as angling scientists, can develop and test hypothesis the same way. We test, explain what we observe, and then refine our theories.

There are two things that modern-day scientists do that make this process more workable. First, they communicate with each other, and secondly, they strive to be absolutely truthful with their observations. Yeah, there have been cases where scientists lied, but when the rest of the scientific community got wind of this, that guy was out of business. Kind of like the fellow who gives you bad info about where and how he catches fish; you just quit listening.

Just think how the angling community would change if we adhered to scientific principles! Who would benefit?
Anglers and fish, that's who.

Chapter One

—◆—

The Angling Environment: "What makes an angler"

"There is a principle which is a bar against all information, which is proof against all arguments and which cannot fail to keep a man in everlasting ignorance—that principle is contempt prior to investigation."

*Herbert Spencer (1820-1903) English philosopher.
(Colleague of Charles Darwin)*

To the uninitiated, fishing conjures images of bobbers and bucolic pond-side naps. No, we're talking about hunting fish and these are the hunters. The best of them know the dawn provides the best opportunity for success.

You can't keep a secret and you know it. You want to tell everyone the saga about how you caught the big one. You notice your fishing friends don't want to hear any of it if they can't hear all of it. Try considering it hunter-gatherer economics. You give them a little, they give you some back. That's how it works, right? And don't think this is a recent phenomenon. There's lots of evidence to suggest it's an ancient practice; some think that missing-link-man got to where he is today by teamwork. It took cooperation with fellow links to migrate and feed themselves.

THE ANGLER AS HUNTER

Folklore and mythology abound regarding the ancient practices of hunting and fishing. Ask anthropologists how ancient man came to inhabit the North American continent and you'll hear about nomadic hunters trekking the frozen Bering Strait land bridge (remember, this is just a theory).

There are other migration theories and one in particular that rings true to me.

Recently, scientists have been digging around the 12,000-year-old remains of an ancient maritime settlement on the coast of Peru. The research indicates that the early North American settlers may have been fishers first, and hunters second.

It makes sense when you think about it.

If you and I were going to try to travel down the North American West Coast from Alaska, I'd suggest the water route. The coastal path presents fewer physical obstructions and we could utilize nature's intertidal seafood-buffet along the way by just picking up a fish, mollusk or gastropod when we felt like it. It sure would beat chasing migrating herds, trekking frozen tundra and traversing mountain ranges.

As archeologists examine the fossil evidence at the Peruvian marine dig, it appears that ancient man actually took the coastal route. Most of the bones and instruments unearthed originated from fish, seabirds, and shellfish.

Physically we have a lot in common with those travelers: same organs, physiology and nutritional requirements. Disregarding technology, culture and philosophy, man is pretty much the same as 12,000 years ago. Our basic drive has always been providing for families and ourselves. Drive is a good description: there are biological consequences if we fail.

What if we anglers fish because we must? We may not have the same immediate needs as the Peruvian maritime settlers, but maybe our evolutionary "wiring" demands it.

Thousands of years ago, this warrior would have sharpened arrows and spears, not hooks.

THE ANGLER AS PHILOSOPHER

In fact, I don't know an angler that hasn't at some time justified their efforts by saying to themselves, "You know, if I had to, I could survive another day by catching fish. . ." Could we be rationalizing our genetic requirement to fish?

I think so. It's even possible that some of non-angler/hunters could be conning themselves by thinking they can fulfill that need in the corporate world or by watching

Catch, admire and release.

sports. "Did you see that contract I just pulled down?" Or, "Yeah man, the Anaheim Mighty Ducks almost got the cup, but the Nashville Predators killed them in the end."

For some of us, that just doesn't cut it. Doesn't satisfy that deep down hunger for fishing, for hunting, for nature... for biological completion. When obsessed anglers are on the water, they're fulfilling millions of years of evolution. Face it, we are animals, albeit often conscious animals. This means that we are aware of what we're doing, or can be. Hopefully we'll use this in our evolutionary game of musical chairs.

A thinking animal understands that he's an animal and acts responsibly. We indulge our need to catch but we temper our instinct to kill. Sure, we could just catch a fish and eat it there on the spot, but our situation isn't that urgent. When we give it thought, we realize that a released fish survives to spawn.

MAN AS MODERN ANGLER

Anglers today are different than they were just 20 years ago. Most are more sophisticated and they want details, not just where you found fish and what you used. No sir, they want to hear the why's and what if's. Once they've caught a few fish, maybe some big ones, the principles behind fish-catching become important. They want to understand fish and a fish's relationship to nature. Today's angler is an inquisitive angler—once again, a scientific angler by inclination.

New Breed of Angler

"I love fishing because it's the only sport where I get to eat my opponent after I win."

Rick Morris (1957-)
Catastrophic insurance claim adjuster,
stand-up comedian

I arrived at the Cabo San Lucas marina at about 5:45 a.m. What I saw reminded me of the bar scene in Star Wars. Instead of raiders from Calderon and Wookies doing deals, there were sportfish hustlers and sportfish hustle-ee's, sleepy-eyed anglers from some flat-sounding place in Texas, and me. I also identified another species of angler, one I've only recently typed out.

It's a new breed.

You'll see them in Montana, Mexico or Madagascar. Just about any aquatic environment. They live to fish. And many of them fish to live. These are not your tweed-and-pipe crowd. No, they're often pierced and goateed now. Mostly nice guys, polite and smart. Kind of like an angling version of the surfers my mother reluctantly tolerated. Call them guides, pro's, angling and outdoor gear mavens, whatever, they're hooked on fishing.

These guys catch a lot of fish. I think it's because they're hunters and somewhat nomadic as they follow the fishing season

year round. They come to Baja for fun. Translated: non-stop shoulder-wrenching, arm-aching, lip-ripping fishing.

Did I mention they're not married? Not that they wouldn't want a feminine influence around, it's just tough to find one committed to towing boats down a decrepit Baja road and

Men and boats. A historical precedence: Vikings, Eskimos, explorers. . . and anglers.

sleeping in the dirt. If there is a woman in the picture, she's usually a newcomer and she doesn't comprehend how deeply pathological this thing of theirs is. Once she does, she'll likely extricate herself from this unnatural three-way love affair: man, fish. . .and, oh yeah, woman.

(I've heard of a few women that have profiles similar to the guys described above, I just haven't had the privilege to meet any. Can you just imagine it: being a young woman, fly-fishing around the world? I bet a few of the boys would tell her where the fish are biting.)

Angling warriors? There's a genetic precedence for this, an abundance of evidence which supports the notion that man is hardwired to hunt. These modes of inherited genetic behavioral characteristics, often referred to as Lamarckian theories, are out of favor today, but there does appear to be something to it.

Behavioral hardwiring might seem to be a rather simplistic approach, but I'll use it anyway. A good example is my dog Buck. He comes from a long line of chocolate lab field trial champions (the specifics of which I will forgo here, but any other time, ask me and I'll bore you to tears). His superior retrieving ability becomes apparent when he's in the water. Seems relatively straightforward for a retriever, Lamarckian or not. Right?

But when it comes to you and I as human beings, the direct effect of genes on behavior gets a little foggy. See, the majority of modern Man's genetic information remains pretty much the same as it's been for hundreds of thousands of years. Most of that time, man hunted. Problem is that nowadays hunting is often inconvenient, usually unnecessary and frequently frowned upon. But ladies, the fact remains, you could probably get guys to go to the supermarket if they could track the groceries and bring them down.

Angling is a "civilized" way for modern man to hunt. Especially catch-and-release angling. We get to stalk, cast to and capture our prey. Then, because we're magnanimous, release the defeated quarry to go back to nature, now a more educated member of their species. Win, win. The fish wise up a little, we get to catch them another day.

Angler Characteristics

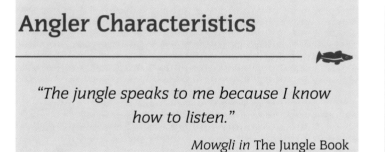

"The jungle speaks to me because I know how to listen."

Mowgli in The Jungle Book

What exactly makes a good angler? Well, that's hard to say for sure.

Initially, I was going to psychologically profile a hundred anglers that were reputed to be better than most. Early on in my investigation I found out that I didn't have to administer tests, I just had to listen and take notes.

Here's what I discovered.

As you might expect, most good anglers are not laid back about fishing. You might describe their level of interest as ranging from really interested to obsessed out of their gourds. As I progressed in my investigation I heard more about individual personalities than reproducible behaviors. When I pressed for particulars, trends in personality and habits surfaced.

For example, most good anglers actually kept some sort of record of their fishing techniques and results (see Chapter 10, Field Guide). I find that while many anglers think it's a good idea, only the better ones actually do it.

FISH OUTSIDE THE BOX

One attribute successful anglers have in common, though not many of them admit to it (which in and of itself may be a characteristic of a good angler), is that they fish innovative places. What I mean by innovative are places that many of us wouldn't think to fish.

A good example of this occurred during a steelhead fishing trip on Vancouver Island with a local guide who is considered by many (including himself) to be the best guide on the island.

Take a peek at a pro's tackle box, make mental notes about colors, individual styles and approaches to angling.

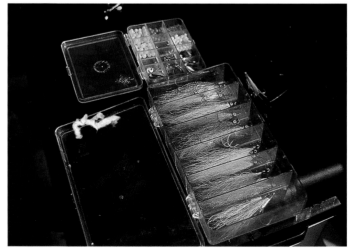

From a morphological perspective, these imitations are uniform with only slight variation in color. This professional angler found an imitation (morphology) that works consistently and is varying the hue qualities for different seasons and conditions.

We took out of the marina and we hadn't traveled a quarter of a mile when we set up shop to fish a steelhead lie. Normally, when you think of British Columbia, you think of pristine wilderness and remote fishing. But this morning we were working water a hundred yards from a freeway overpass with the noise of the morning Port Alberni rush hour as a backdrop. I asked him what on earth made him think this was potentially good or innovative place to fish. He replied, "Everyone knows there's no fish here because it's so accessible." That morning we caught 15 fish before noon.

There are two points here: think critically about what you believe, and try different places.

COMMUNICATION IS LISTENING

Good anglers talk to experts and actively listen to them. Now that may seem obvious but it's not. Anglers would like to think they learn from others' experience. What I've observed is often just the opposite: most anglers, while appearing to listen, are just waiting for their turn to talk. Their agenda is to impress the expert with what they know.

It seems that the experts don't need to say much; they become the listeners. I wonder if that's how they became experts?

ANGLING FAITH

Good anglers believe in their equipment and expect fish to be there. If you adopt this attitude, your gear will be in the water longer. As a result, your lure stays in the fish-impact zone more and increases your chances of catching fish. This just makes sense. In my own experience, I've found that changing lures or flies every 30 seconds and moving from spot to spot, before I've adequately worked a section, often comes from doubting my strategy and equipment.

Fly-fishing in commercial harbors is out of the norm. To achieve better results than most, you have to look "outside the box" and fish unusual places.

Chapter Two

—◄═▶—

The Aquatic Environment

"Highest good is like water. Because water excels in benefiting the myriad creatures without

contending with them and settles where none would like to be, it comes closest to the way."

Lao Tzu, Tao te Ching

The piscine form: exquisitely adapted to its thick aqueous environment. Nature, cheered on by natural selection, created what aeronautical engineers spend entire careers imitating but never duplicating.

It's shortsighted to think about fish as separate from the environment they're in. Fish and water are like opposite sides of the same coin. When you understand different types of water, you've learned a lot about fish.

I've been told that you can't catch migratory fish that you can't see. Well, maybe you don't have to see fish, just fishy water. Once you learn how to read water, fish that were only figments of your imagination will soon wind up on the end of your line.

To fish, water is ubiquitous; so as a fish, you really wouldn't notice it. All you would care about is what it does for you. Water allows you to breathe. Yessir, fish breathe just like humans; it's just that their atmosphere is thicker than ours and it has more mass, both of which have their own physiological consequences.

The increased density of water explains a lot about fish. Like why salmonids are shaped like bullets (see photo). Nature came up with this foiled silhouette to help overcome the friction of sustained swimming.

Air presents the same type of physical constraint to motion. One look at jet aircraft and you'd think that aeronautical engineers took great pains to make their designs resemble trout. (In particular, a Boeing 757 looks like a pregnant brown.) Not that they actually tried to imitate fish, no, that would be too easy. It's just that nature designed fish with their slippery shape to overcome a key property common to both gaseous and aquatic environments, friction.

To a fish, friction is a drag.

THEREIN LIES THE RUB: FRICTION

Pick up any treatise on fishing and you'll see a description of the most likely spots a fish will lie. What exactly determines their preference?

Answer: overcoming friction.

It's most important for a fish to minimize its effort in acquiring food, in order that the energy costs of prehending prey is offset by the nutritional value of the meal. The professional science crowd calls this the "forage optimization theory." You and I can remember it by the "better to put more in the nutritional bank account than you spend from it" theory.

This becomes critical in moving water, where fish must expend energy just to stay even. Fish seek out the areas that have slow-moving water adjacent to swifter currents. This puts them close to the action where they snack on insects and other "fast" foods in the drift.

THE BIG DADDY WATER QUALITY PARAMETER: TEMPERATURE

For fish, temperature is the Numero Uno water-quality parameter and they stay within specific ranges, depending on the species. (see Fish Comfort Zones). If they don't, they die, so they'll do anything to find their optimal temperature comfort zone.

From a global perspective and even from a neighborhood point of view, if you determine the water temperature, you can predict the most likely location of certain species of fish. And it's all because of the way fish evolved.

Over time, species evolved to take advantage of more resources and territory within their physiologically acceptable temperature range. One theory has it that prehistoric salmon were strictly freshwater fish and eventually took to the sea to

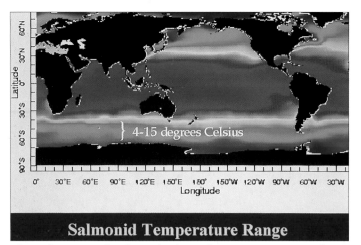

{ 4-15 degrees Celsius

Salmonid Temperature Range

Thermal Zones. Each color in the thermal zones represents specific temperature ranges. When an angler knows a fish's temperature comfort zone, he can predict where they'll be geographically, whether on a continent or in your backyard watershed.

Species	S.E.T. (^{0}C)*	Ideal Temperature Range (^{0}F)
Bass, Largemouth		59-81
Bass, Smallmouth		77-79
Bass, Striped		64-75
Trout, Rainbow	15 (59^{0}F)	
Trout, Brown	15 (59^{0}F)**	
Trout, Brook	15 (59^{0}F)	
Pike, Northern		41-55
Walleye		60-70
Salmon (Pacific)	12 (53.6^{0}F)	
*S.E.T.: Standard Environmental Temperature=Optimal Growth Temperature		
** Brown Trout do better than Rainbows at higher temperatures, but given a choice, they like 59^0 F.		

The key to using temperatures with fishing is when you catch a fish, record the water temperature. Then you have a thermal baseline from which to work. Develop your own database of angling temperatures.

avail themselves of all the marine goodies the ocean provided. To a salmon, this would be logged as "Survival tip #39: expand your domain as far as possible in order to ensure your survivability as a species."

Darwinian take-home message: if a species doesn't adapt to take advantage of its environment, it dies. A good example of this is the trout versus bass phenomenon (see below).

AND THE WINNER IS...

In the trout family, brown trout (*Salmo trutta*) are considered better adapted than rainbow trout (*Oncorhynchus mykiss*). The main reason they do better is because they can tolerate more stress, like slightly warmer water for example. They're also tougher than rainbows when it comes to things like resisting diseases and the effects of encroaching civilization. In the salmonid Fortune 500, this puts brown trout on top but they're no match for warmwater species like bass, perch, pike and muskies.

Bass are farther up the fish food chain from trout. They're tough characters. Put a bass in just about any freshwater situation and they'll do okay (except for on Dan Ackroyd/Lorraine Newman's "Saturday Night Live" Bass-o-Matic commercials). Put bass and trout together and you'll wind up with only a few big bass. As a species, they have a much broader temperature

comfort zone and can out-compete a trout any day. I've seen these fish together in the same water system and it's not pretty.

From an angling point of view, if I'm fishing anyplace where bass (often smallmouth) and trout coexist, I think temperature. Expect trout to be in the faster, colder areas. Look for all species of freshwater bass in the slower warmer water, particularly where there's vegetative cover, structure and drop-offs.

Just because the temperature is suitable for a fish doesn't mean you'll always find them there. But it does mean that if you find water that's out of a species' tolerance range, you're unlikely to find your quarry. The reason you won't find fish out of their range is because there's not adequate dissolved oxygen for their specific needs. Temperature dictates how much O_2 is in the water and that's ultimately what's important to a fish.

CHILL OUT

Fish are ectotherms, meaning they regulate their body temperatures by swimming towards temperatures that suit their tolerances. (Exceptions are some scombroid tuna that are able to keep parts of their muscles warm, and billfish with occular muscles that act as brain heaters.) In general, fish don't generate a lot of body heat like mammals do, and what heat they do create is quickly lost from their gills to the aquatic environment via the heat-sink (absorbing) characteristics of water.

Because water has a tendency to hold its temperature, rapid changes don't happen readily. When dramatic underwater temperature shifts do occur, it's aquatic Armageddon. Swings much more than one degree Centigrade (or 1.8 degrees F.) an hour are a problem. However, fish will survive a mild chill better than sudden warming. A prime example of a well-tolerated cold swing is seen in tailwater fisheries where dams release cool flows from the reservoir bottom.

All this just reinforces our mantra: "fish the temperatures."

SOMETHING'S IN THE AIR

As human beings, we don't often have a conscious appreciation for oxygen. Except under unusual circumstances, like emphysema, we take O_2 for granted. This is primarily because we terrestrials evolved where the air's plentiful. But imagine for a moment, how it might effect our coming and going if we experienced geographical areas of reduced air availability, much like a fish experiences varying oxygen concentrations in different areas and types of water.

Visualize yourself as a fish, driving down the piscatorial freeway on a hot day. Suddenly you notice that it's hard to breathe, "maybe it's an asthma attack", you say to yourself. Panicky, you exit at the next off-ramp adjacent to a cool turbulent spring and you immediately begin to breathe a little easier. "Whew, glad that's over," you think, "I'll just hang out here near this spring mouth...maybe wait for some food to come by." What's your assessment of this place? Its got everything going for it: easier to breathe, less work swimming and there's a quick escape route too. Well, now you're thinking like a fish. Note again, your first priority was getting oxygen from the cool spring and not having to swim hard to get it.

THE MARRIAGE OF OXYGEN AND TEMPERATURE

Oxygen and temperature are linked. As the temperature climbs, waters' capacity to hold oxygen diminishes because the dissolved gas expands and vaporizes into the atmosphere. That's why we were running short of breath on the hot fish freeway in the first place.

KEY POINT HERE: WARM WATER CONTAINS LESS OXYGEN.
In general it's true. Warmer water does contain less oxygen but that doesn't mean cold water always has more. Water from underground aquifers is usually pretty cold but because of the biological processes (bacteria, etc.) that occur as the water percolates through the ground, there may be no O_2. In addition, deep lakes and other bodies of water are anoxic (low oxygen) in the colder deep reaches because the biological activity there (plankton, algae and decaying vegetable matter) consumes what little oxygen there is.

Cold anoxic water doesn't always have to remain low in oxygen. In great tailwater fisheries, the water is anoxic as it comes out of the reservoir bottom but readily absorbs atmospheric oxygen via the mechanical agitation of the dam. In turbulent rivers and streams, the water's oxygen concentration is often near saturation because a similar mixing phenomenon created by the stream's rocks and boulders.

Sometimes water can become supersaturated with dissolved gases (e.g. nitrogen) near a dam or waterfall. When the jet-like action of water absorbs higher than normal concentrations of atmospheric gas, the water becomes supersaturated. This situation causes all sorts of problems for fish like "gas bubble disease." So look a little downstream towards the riffles instead of the hydroelectric turbines, before you expect to find fish.

AND HEREIN LIES AN ANGLING TIP:
SEEK FISH IN AREAS OF HIGH OXYGEN CONTENT.
Of special note are calm waters adjacent to turbulent (or moving) ones. Fish like to lie in the slower-moving water while poking their noses into the faster, more oxygen-rich currents flowing by.

FIELD TRIP
If you examine the anatomy of a typical stream you'll find a few constants. Most creeks and rivers have the typical components of riffles, runs and pools, all with varying levels of water agitation or turbulence. Again, turbulent water is well-aerated water with a high dissolved oxygen content. If oxygen were the only thing of importance to a fish, you'd think they'd spend all their time there, but there are other things to consider.

For example, a fish has to constantly weigh whether the effort expended is worth it or not. We know a fish will lie in a seam where there is well-oxygenated faster-flowing water within reach. In all actuality, the dissolved oxygen on both sides of the interface will be the same (most likely something near 6 or 7 PPM O_2) but may differ significantly from other areas of the stream. Later in the season, for example, calmer waters approach the upper temperature tolerances and oxygen depletion comes into play.

Usually the water coming through a riffle is well oxygenated and loaded with insects. But in pools things change. The head of the pool has the best oxygen and provides prime foraging opportunities. This is where you'll find the dominant fish, not always the biggest, just the bossiest alpha-attitudes.

Whether you're fishing for record stripers or northern coho, expect fish to be attracted to side inlets that provide favorable temperature and oxygen conditions. Fish can be above, but often below, where a side inlet enters a main body of water. This side inlet enters an Alaskan river (upper right). Remember that there can be numerous inlets and outlets, sometimes underground. See if the landscaping and terrain gives you any clues to their location.

Another good spot to find fish is at the confluence of a side stream or underground spring. Here fish can manage their temperature and select dinner from the invertebrate drift of insects.

Angling tip: look for fish where water enters another body of water...e.g. head of pool, side inlets.

Seabirds working tell you where the fish are. Birds often key on baitfish breaking the surface. If you can't see the baitfish, "nervous water" appearance on the surface, sometimes the birds will tell you where the bait is (and the sportfish that love them).

Both glassy pools and rippled waters have distinctive water quality characteristics (temperature, oxygen, etc.). Fish know this and take advantage of it. Famous for its pools, this spot on the Beaverkill, near Roscoe, New York, has similar aquatic properties to pools in many anglers' "back yards."

THE UPS AND DOWNS OF SEAMS

I'm going to make this real easy. Now, remember, any time someone makes something real easy, there are going to be exceptions. I know this because my wife, Jan, is an expert at pointing out the exceptions to any generalizations I make (a.k.a. "Jan's Rule"). Undaunted, I proceed.

Gaining an understanding of seams is simple: fish are lazy. They're underachievers who won't do a thing unless there's something in it for them and it's a relatively sure deal. They want the best of both worlds, I call this "life in the seams."

Fish enjoy seams because if you're a fish, this is where the action is. Fish like to eat, protect their territory, find dates, and, for lack of a better word, loiter. (Similar to teenagers at the mall.)

I categorize seams two ways: vertical and horizontal.

VERTICAL AND HORIZONTAL SEAMS

Vertical seams occur where currents of different speeds interface. You can distinguish vertical seams on the surface by looking at their edges, like books on a library shelf. They're found in both fresh and marine environments; wherever moving water

Moving water impacting an obstruction will produce vertical seams. There are vertical seams on most aspects of this rock. Expect to find fish "surfing the cushion" in front of the rock and "drafting the eddy" behind it. Both these vertical hydrodynamic phenomena are utilized by fish to conserve energy and observe drifting prey.

Horizontal seams are somewhat tricky to grasp. If the bottom isn't flat, the contours, projections and depressions all serve to trap or accelerate the laminar (horizontally oriented and sheet-like) characteristics of water. Look for fish in the holes and depressions (dark areas), which lie under the faster moving sheets of water.

flows against physical contours or drops from the shallows into deeper reaches. Boulders and other objects that divert current, create vertical seams as well.

Horizontal seams, on the other hand, are often hidden from our view. Think of them as laminar water layers, like a Jell-O parfait or one of those three-story Cabo San Lucas cocktails. A fish lying in a depression is really taking advantage of a horizontal seam. The slower water in the hole requires less energy expenditure, while the faster water above provides assorted prey items; and this position allows for a good vantagepoint to pick off approaching predators.

COMBINATION OF VERTICAL AND HORIZONTAL

As water impacts a rock, a horizontal cushion or wave of water develops on the upstream aspect. A fish holding here is actually pushed forward into the oncoming current (surf's up). Behind the rock, a "V"-shaped vertical seams, called an eddy, also provides fish with places where they can "coast" with a minimum of effort while still surveilling the passing prey parade.

You can get a feel for an eddy yourself by tailgating a semi-truck on the freeway at 60 mph. You'll notice when you get within a few car lengths that you're sucked into the truck's "slipstream."

Once you get within one car length, you're actually using about half the amount of gas as would be otherwise necessary to maintain your vehicle speed. That's presuming you survive the experiment! (I strongly discourage trying this, otherwise you could end up discovering the freeway version of a horizontal seam: i.e. under the truck.)

UPWELLING SEAMS

Finding fish in the ocean can be difficult. This is due to the fact that most of the ocean is barren. Although the majority of marine organisms live within the boundaries of the continental shelf (200 miles from shore), it's still a vast area—and fish move around a lot.

Most of my ocean fishing is estuarine (where freshwater enters brackish or saltwater) and conducted relatively close to shore. It's in these areas that I've identified another seam potentially useful to anglers: phosphorus seams. You can recognize these by their foamy appearance. The foam consists of phosphorus-containing organic materials that's pushed to the surface by upwelling currents that contains phytoplankton and zooplankton (tiny creatures on which baitfish feed).

Because sportfish follow and feed on baitfish, phosphorus seams are a tip off to the angling action.

SALINITY SEAMS

You can't always easily see valuable angling areas. For example, you might think that salt water and fresh water would look the same, but fish sure can tell the difference. And if you know what to look for, you can see seams where salt water meets fresh water. Look for a difference in light refraction where the fresh water inflows mix with salt water in an estuary. (See photo.) What you'll see is a "frosted glass" appearance at the interface of the two water types. This frosted look or slight opacity, is due to differences in light diffraction amongst the varying salinity contents.

Salinity seams are important, because that's where you'll have a good chance to catch a nice coastal cutthroat and other migratory species. Cuttys (cutthroat trout) haunt these edges because with each tide they find new dietary opportunities. A

Areas of foam accumulation indicate phosphorus seams. The upwelling of currents carries phytoplankton, zooplankton and other organic materials from the ocean depths. These foamy seams have high nutritional value for baitfish. Look for baitfish and sportfish here.

rising tide, combined with turbulent stream runoff, dislodges invertebrates and the occasional hapless fry. Fresh water contains more oxygen than salt water (at the same temperature), so here we have again, that winning combination of lots of oxygen to breathe and plenty to eat.

I find that salinity seams produce best right after a high tide, which makes good fish-foraging sense.

TEMPERATURE SEAMS
Lastly, seams allow fish ways to thermoregulate (manage their body temperature). We know they do this by moving to one side of the seam or the other, along a water-temperature gradient, while always retaining the ability to flee from danger. If a predator approaches from the bank, the faster moving water on the cooler side of the seam provides a quick escape route in addition to cooling off.

Angling tip: fish the seams.

Anglers are used to thinking about seams in freshwater environments. Marine environments provide a new context. Upwelling currents can be thought of as a type of seam that brings the promise of the depths to within flyfishing range.

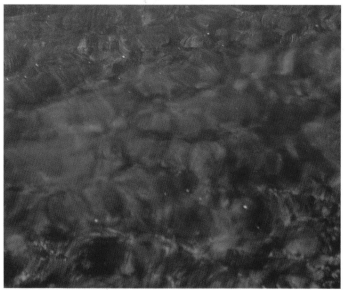

Salinity seams are amorphous refractive distortions in water. You'll find these in estuaries where fresh water mixes with its marine counterpart. The result is a "frosted-glass" appearance to the water. Salinity seams are highly sought after by migrating estuarine species like coastal cutthroat trout and rainbows. In the Pacific Northwest, these seams are often associated with oyster beds and dense benthic (bottom-dwelling) marine life.

Swimbladders

"The illustration of the swim-bladder in fishes is a good one, because it shows us clearly the highly important fact that an organ originally constructed for one purpose, namely, flotation, may be converted into one for a widely different purpose, namely respiration. . . All physiologists admit that the swim-bladder is homologous, or "ideally similar" in position and structure with the lungs of the higher vertebrate animals: hence there is no reason to doubt that the swim-bladder has actually been converted into lungs, or an organ used exclusively for respiration."

Charles Darwin, The Origin of Species, 1859

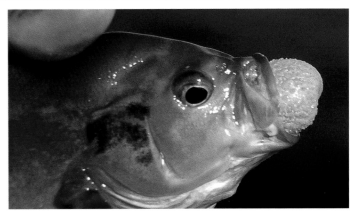

Air bladders protrude because of the rapid expansion of organ gas—caused by retrieving fish to the surface from moderate depths (usually greater than 30 feet).

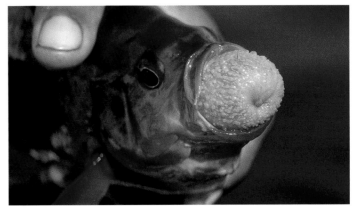

A quick hook-prick on the prolapsed (protruding) swimbladder, and the fish was ready to go back to the depths.

Swim bladders (a.k.a. gas bladders, air bladders) are just weird organs. They remind me of something you'd see in a superhero cartoon.

Sea Robin:	BatFishMan! We must ascend the water column!
BatfishMan:	Great Gas Pains! Deploy the Batbladders!
Sea Robin:	Ahhhmm. . . Are we allowed to do that, so soon after eating?

But who needs fiction when you have science? Swimbladders are amazing aquatic airbags that adjust the fish's buoyancy, allowing them to travel up and down the vertical feeding column.

"What's the big deal, why don't they just swim?"

Easy for you to say but that's akin to treading water your whole life.

One of the important ways the aquatic environment is different from our terrestrial environment, is that water's a lot denser than air which makes it harder to be mobile. A fish has got to get around both horizontally and vertically.

Human beings ran around in animal skin loincloths for millennia before we dealt with the vertical component of space by inventing airplanes. Fish didn't have to design aircraft, they became them (or the aquatic version, anyway). And of all flying machines, fish most resemble dirigibles.

SWIMBLADDER SCHEMATICS

Swim bladders come in two varieties, physoclistous or physostomous. If the organ has a connecting duct to the esophagus (physostomous), the fish can belch out accumulated gas. On the other fin, if a species deals with gas volume changes by way of diffusion (physoclistous), they must leak the gas slowly into the bloodstream.

Marvelous as they may be, don't think that having a swim bladder is always a day at the beach. A major downside with some species' airbags is depicted in the photo of a snapper retrieved from 50 feet. What you see demonstrates a basic design flaw of almost Hindenberg proportions: certain fish can't handle quick ascents. If forced to do so, as when winched to the surface by some mammal on a party boat, their bladder acts like helium-filled balloons rising unrestricted, expanding until a real problem emerges (right out the mouth). Such uncompensated swim bladder expansion will prevent a fish from returning to depth when released. Not only can this phenomona kill a fish, it is in scientific terms, "distressing"; ergo, this condition is named Swimbladder Distress Syndrome (SBDS).

Is it always terminal?

Nope.

How do you spell relief?

P U N C T U R E.

Yep, that's right, just pop it. If the swim bladder is protruding from the mouth, all you have to do is take an 18-gauge (or so) hypodermic needle and puncture the bladder. When it deflates, you can release the fish. If you don't have a hypodermic needle handy (which you can get from a feed store), you can puncture

Whether bass, rockfish or tuna, many sportfish have swimbladders. In this example, Mother Nature's hydrodynamic design criterion of albacore is evident even at the abdominal organ level. Here we see the tapered, bullet-shaped air bladder of a Pacific albacore. Below the bladder lies the pink stomach (that contained a squid) adjacent to the maroon/brown liver.

it with a sharp pick or big canvas needle. Personally, I recommend puncturing before resorting to cutting with a knife because a puncture wound will seal itself better than a knife-tip laceration. Lacerations (slits, cuts, etc.) can lead to swimbladder bacterial infections, which are another bummer for fish.

If the bladder isn't protruding from the mouth, which is often the case with deeply retrieved black bass, you can use the hypodermic needle to deflate the swim bladder from a side approach, as detailed in the photo of the largemouth bass bladder deflation. This is a little dicey, but with a little practice it can be done safely.

Traveling the vertical dimension isn't the only thing accomplished by these aquatic animals. Thick, cold, unpredictable water. You never know if it's going to be cloudy or clear. How do fish know where to go, given that water can be such a poor medium for sensing?

We've all heard about sensory-disabled humans who compensated by enhancing other senses. Same with fish. And swim bladders are just what the doctor ordered! Not only do they allow fish to efficiently travel vertically, but they also augment underwater hearing by functioning as a supersensitive, vibration-receiving drum.

When it comes to specialized organ-receiving drums, freshwater bass have ones that are hard to beat (see sidebar "Good Vibrations," pg. 46). Bass evolved in visually restricted environments, filled with murky dark-algae-laden water. Over time,

they've come to rely on their swimbladders more than most, evolving theirs into a highly developed, vibration-sensing hearing device.

SUMMARY: DEALING WITH SWIMBLADDER DISTRESS SYNDROME.

If the swimbladder is protruding from the mouth, a small puncture will do the trick. When you release the fish, it'll be able to resume its preferred depth.

Don't use a knife if you can use a pick, needle or some other sharp-pointed cylindrical object. A debarbed hook will often do the trick if you straighten it out with a pair of pliers.

Swimbladder Distress Syndrome in bass can be treated by percutaneous decompression with an 18-gauge needle. (The cutaway view is for illustration purposes only).

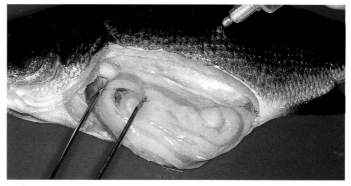

You can reuse your 18-gauge needle, but store it in a little rubbing alcohol to avoid introducing bacteria into the next patient's swimbladder.

Seamless Lake Fishing

"Flow with whatever is happening and let your mind be free. Stay centered by accepting whatever you are doing. This is the ultimate."

Chuang Tzu

Lakes and ponds are serene, peaceful. Not much really going on. OK, there's the occasional waterfowl and wild animal (beavers, water-skiers. . .), but otherwise not much else. How do we know there's any fish in there? And if there were a few they could be anywhere, right?

Wrong!

It's actually easier to predict where fish will be in lakes than just about any other body of water. Just look for the seams. . .

LAKES 101

A basic understanding of limnology (limnos = pool, lake or swamp and logos = discourse or field of study), as it pertains to lakes, tells the whole story. Water stratifies in lakes or ponds. This

Float tubing dawn patrol on the stillwater watch.

means the heavy (cold and dense) water sinks to the bottom, lighter (warm, less dense) water floats on the top. And when the lake water is the same temperature (and therefore the same density), it mixes around. That's all there is to it, right? Well, not exactly.

OXYGEN REVIEW

We know that there's a direct relationship between dissolved oxygen and the water's temperature. And if a fish has to choose, it'll always go for oxygen over temperature. Also remember that the warmer the water, the less oxygen. Conversely, the colder the water the more oxygen it contains, unless the water is too deep for sunlight to reach the plant life that produces oxygen via photosynthesis.

COOL EXTERIOR

In a lake, the coldest water is always on the bottom, with one exception. This is the last exception, I promise. Cold water is always on the bottom until it reaches 4° Celsius (about 40° Fahrenheit) where it becomes lighter and floats upward. As it continues to cool, it solidifies into ice when it nears 0° C (32° F).

But in general, unless you're into ice fishing, the warmest water is on the top, coldest on the bottom.

LAKE LAMINATIONS

The three layers of a lake are collectively called isotherms. They are individually named, from top to bottom: Epilimnion (epi = on or upon, limnion = lake or pool), Metalimnion (Meta = beyond) the in-between section, also known as the thermocline, and the Hypolimnion (you guessed it, Hypo = under... I told you this wasn't rocket science), which is on the bottom.

Fish seek their species-specific comfort zones within the thermal layers of the lake (isotherms). Infrequently, fish will venture outside their preferred temperature range but only because the cool water is so far down it's anoxic or all the prey is located in the warmer extremes.

You can see this during the warm summer months when the epilimnion deepens its range due to prolonged sun exposure.

A scientific angler will want to keep a thermometer on a measurement cord handy so the exact depth of the temperature comfort zone, and the fish we seek, can be identified. Remember that fish apprehend prey for a living. They want to hunt in comfort. But their prey doesn't always share the same idea of what's home. That means that the place to find fish is where the thermal comfort zone intersects their prey's habitat.

Aquatic prey follow all the rules in lakes that you observe in other bodies of water. You'll find benthic prey (bottom-dwellers) on the bottom and you'll see small baitfish in the vegetative habitat that coincides within their specific temperature preferences. This plant area is formally called the littoral zone, which is where you'll discover adequate cover such as boulders, aquatic vegetation, trees and other structure. Again, remember to look for cool underground springs as a source of temperature-preferred water even though the surrounding water is warmer than desired. I usually find the inlet and outlets of a lake or pond being the best angling zones in lakes.

Angling tip: First, find the temperature seams. Second, find the seams of prey habitat. Lastly, find where they intersect each other and adjust your drag.

SUMMARY: KEY PROPERTIES OF WATER THAT ANGLERS NEED TO KNOW

Water gets denser (heavier) as it gets colder until it reaches 40 Celsius. (I don't know why... ask the molecules.)

Water gets lighter when it gets colder than 40 Celsius, this is why ice floats.

Water in lakes has layers like the laminations in a sheet of plywood.

Wind mixes up the layers when the layers have the same temperature (late spring and late fall).

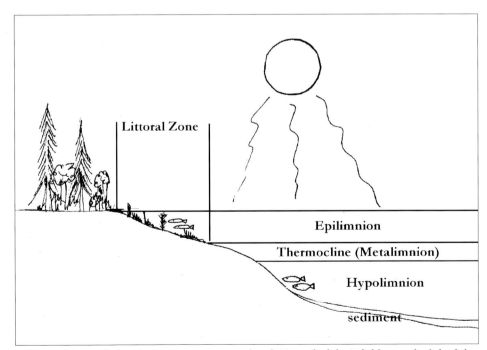

Lakes stratify into layers that are temperature related. Most of a lake is fishless, so look for fish where the temperatures and habitat are the most likely to produce.

Inlets and outlets to stillwater bodies provide great opportunities for fish to take advantage of potential prey. The transition from inlet to lake, or lake to outlet, provides for physical contours (structure) for both prey and predators. Target these areas any time for fish.

Get Edgy

"Water dives from the clouds without parachute, wings or safety net. Water runs over the steepest precipice and blinks not a lash. Water is buried and rises again; water walks on fire and fire gets the blisters. Stylishly composed in any situation—solid, gas or liquid—speaking in penetrating dialects understood by all things—animal, vegetable or mineral—water travels intrepidly through four dimensions, sustaining. . . destroying. . . creating. . ."

—Tom Robbins,
from the preface to Even Cowgirls Get the Blues

THE DIFFERENCE BETWEEN FISH AND CRIMINALS

Willie Sutton was a New York City bank robber. When interviewed on TV during a prison hiatus, there was an especially poignant moment when he stated why he robbed banks. Willie stated matter-of-factly "because that's where the money is." Hmmm...

The place to find any predator (fish or crook) is to go where the resources are. It doesn't matter whether you're observing the pinstriped variety on Wall Street, or zebras drinking from a Serengeti riverbank, find the resource and you'll find the opportunist. Fish are no exception. They're in it for the resources, just like you and I. For them this translates to food, oxygen, shelter, and reproduction.

Contrast in geography provides resources for invertebrates, baitfish and predators alike. Seams created by water flow, temperature or salinity create differences in velocity, temperature or salinity concentrations. The contour of the water's shoreline and bottom creates physical contrasts, which an angler can take advantage of by utilizing charts, like the nautical ones provided by NOAA.

WATCH THAT FIRST STEP

Grab your chart and look for drop-offs. Sudden depth changes provide the trifecta of evolutionary rewards: prey, protection and partners. Prey, like baitfish, like steep drop-offs because on

Topo maps and NOAA (National Oceanic and Atmospheric Administration) charts provide a wealth of information to anglers. Used together, you can get information on drop-offs, depths and the most likely fish-holding water.

one side, the shallow water provides a great place for them to eat the aquatic organisms they feed on (shrimp, scuds, etc.) and on the other, the deeper water provides protection from predators above.

But woe to the stickleback that gets too close to the edge at the wrong time! He winds up in the same fix as low-I.Q. seals frolicking in the surf-line, easy pickins for picnicing Orcas.

CHILL OUT

Edges and drop-offs also provide temperature relief for fish, places where they can regulate their body temperature by moving to water that's within their optimal range. During morning's low light, when ambient temperature is coolest, the shallow side of a drop-off is a great place for piscine hunters to apprehend prey while still staying relatively safe from their own enemies. As the sun ascends and the day warms, a fish's enemies (like herons) are more likely to approach the water's edge. Then the same hunting fish move towards deeper, cooler and more secure water.

Knowing about this early morning and late evening migration helps anglers catch fish, or it should. (I am embarrassed to admit how many times I've inadvertently spooked big fish in the shallows at dawn, as I'm bushwhacking my way to the bank like Sasquatch before his first cup of coffee.)

Angling tip: Look for fish in the shallows at dawn and dusk and you'll find them.

ANGLING CARTOGRAPHY

Get dialed into geographical drop-offs by combining US Forestry Service topo maps with the NOAA maps. With this you can see where the area's watersheds (the hillside streams, creeks and lakes) intersect with the larger bodies of water as depicted on the NOAA maps. Getting this overview will allow you to identify areas that likely contain underground springs and channels. (Sometimes these are obvious, especially on NOAA maps.) It's useful to know the locations of these features because their temperatures often differ from the surrounding areas. Sometimes they're warmer, like the hot springs on the Firehole in Yellowstone National Park, but usually cooler, often by as much as 10-15° F, which makes them popular places to hold during summer heat.

As you've surely noted, there's often a risk to hunting: getting eaten in the process. This phenomenon goes by the name "foraging-predation risk trade-off" (sounds like it was defined by my sister-in-law Beverly, the CPA).

"Sure," you say, "And I suppose there's research to show that fish take risk into account when they're chasing prey?"

Well yes, there is, I'm glad you asked!

Scientists discovered that juvenile coho salmon are less willing to stray far from refuge in order to intercept floating prey if they're presented with photographs of large predatory trout (their natural predators).

Most of us can identify with that. Human beings aren't much different from juvenile coho.

Socrates, in his prisoners-in-the-cave allegory, described how men are held captive by images of guards, which were, in fact, nothing more than their own shadows cast on the cave's wall. Even cattle won't cross the road if there are white lines painted to resemble a potential foot trap.

Nope, people aren't much different from cows or coho. No one likes to take undue risks.

Angling tip: Fish won't take undue risks to apprehend prey. Look for refuge as promising holding water.

Marine environments are analogous in many ways to freshwater terrain. Rocky reef areas and vegetation (kelp beds) provide refuge and food sources for prey items like baitfish, which predatory sportfish find irresistible.

Chapter Three

Fish Hardware

"Anatomy is destiny."

— *Sigmund Freud*

Regardless of species, the piscine visual system is a must to understand to become truly versed in the science of angling.

How's it feel to have a sturgeon as a cousin?

From a paleontological point of view, it wasn't that long ago that the terrestrial (us) and aquatic species (fish) were cousins via a common ancestor. All it took was one airborne gasp and mammals, reptiles, insects and other creatures were destined to homestead terra firma while the sea-borne individuals stayed behind and explored the oceans. As our Paleozoic parentage parted company, each dealt with life through evolution, just in much different environments.

Our underwater relatives developed the means to efficiently extract oxygen from H_2O and travel in it well enough to acquire food and create territory. They did this by evolving gills and unique environmental sensing organs that allowed life in an aqueous environment.

As anglers, we're primarily interested in these marvelous physiological adaptations because of what they tell us about fish, especially when they offer clues about where to find them and how to catch them. Some of the most interesting sensory systems are vision, hearing and smell (or taste).

Each one of these systems is exquisitely arranged and developed to function in an environment that's much different from ours. Fish were forced to develop abilities, which to us seem quite foreign.

Overstated you think?

Try to imagine oxygen superchargers that light up the piscine visual system allowing enhanced sight in low light (see sidebar pg. 30). Consider pressure sensitivity so great, that if we had such ability, you and I could from our living room couch, literally feel someone walking up our driveway. If you had the olfactory (smelling)

abilities of a fish you could smell soup simmering for dinner and know that it needed more salt.

Right now a good question to ask is, "How does this guy know what fish experience?"

Not being a piscine psychic, I can't report from verbal accounts. But what you and I can do is make logical inferences from a fish's physiological hardware: a form of "reverse engineering."

For example, if a fish has eyes it must see or if a fish has taste buds, it must taste. As you reduce this down to the very basic of systems, it doesn't take a rocket scientist to get the drift of the fish experience.

FISH EYES

Probably the best place to embark on a discussion of the sensory equipment of sportfish is a perusal of the piscine visual system. Fish eyes are designed to function in an aquatic environment. Things happen fast in watery environments, so you, as a fish, must make quick decisions. You also can't ponder potential meals for very long, since a leisurely study leaves you vulnerable to attack from predators.

The piscine eye is an optical monitor that allows a fish to respond quickly, usually along the lines of "Go" or "No-go." The image of prey, whether authentic or our imitation, is viewed and acted upon in fractions of a second.

This isn't how we function visually as humans. While shopping for produce we muse and peruse, view and thump melons from different perspectives. We gather as much information as we can. Our retinas' densely-packed rods and cones allow for detailed discrimination and discernment of objects.

Most fish can't take the time to be this picky, everything's life or death with them. Whether a fish is in a hyaline (saltwater)

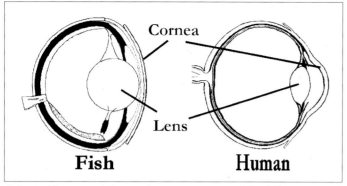

Spherical lenses and flattened corneas are two of the differences between fish eyes and ours.

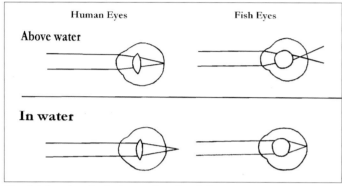

The fish lens is spherical enough to bend the aquatic image to a convergent focal point on the retina, where a human lens can't (humans looking under water unaided are farsighted, or a condition of hyperopia). Conversely, in air, the fish lens bends the image too much (fish becomes nearsighted, or myopia) so the image focuses too far in front of the retina.

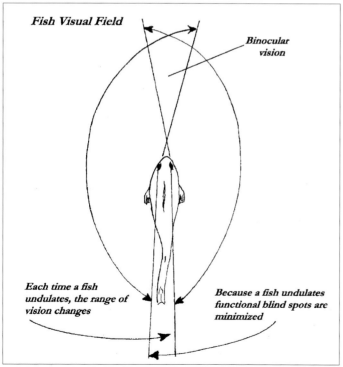

Fish have a wide range of binocular vision in front of them, allowing good depth perception. Undulations minimize blind spots.

environment, fresh water or somewhere in-between (euryhyaline), it's always the same question: how does this potential prey-object look in relationship to the environment? Said from a fish-perspective, "Given everything else I'm used to seeing, is this object different...and could it be...prey?"

Exactly how fish glean this information depends on their visual hardware. First, let's look at the way they see, then we'll look at some specific applications to angling.

EYE PLACEMENT

Most sportfish have their eyes planted on each side of their head (lateral placement). This creates the ability to see a widely arced field of vision (see diagram). A lot has been said about fish having visual "blind spots." Sure, fish in straightjackets have them, and so do a few bottom-dwellers. But these aren't functional blind spots, because fish undulate with coordinated eye movements that produce overlapping visual fields. Without this kind of compensatory feature, nature (e.g. predators) would have a deadly advantage.

Some fish have dorsally-oriented eyes, like the northern pike in the photo. This is a useful adaptation for a "lie-in-wait" predator because it can lurk in the vegetative bottom and take

A lie-in-wait predator, the northern pike's eyes are crocodilian in appearance and serve much the same function as its reptilian resemblance.

advantage of the unsuspecting prey above—like those swimming in formation behind Mama. Baby ducks are a favorite morsel for these masters of ambush, so lures representing demur feathered waterfowl and small furred meat-sticks imitations are consistent producers.

CORNEA AND LENS

Once light reflected from an object reaches the fish, it passes through the cornea into the anterior eye chamber, traverses the lens and eventually impacts the retina. Then the image becomes neurologically converted to a chemical impulse that is "interpreted" by the brain. How images are decoded depends on what a fish has learned (see Chapter 6 Behavior) and by the tissues (cornea, lens, retina etc.) the image comes in contact with.

LET'S COMPARE

When we humans look under water unaided, features appear blurred because the optical properties of water cause images to focus behind our retinas, as if we were farsighted (hyperopia). Fish can see well in water, but if suddenly airborne become nearsighted (myopia) because images focus in front of their retinas.

If form follows function, then this hammerhead depends a lot on vision because its cephalic (head) structure is primarily designed to support its ocular systems.

The chinook salmon's lens is smaller than the shark's and also smaller in proportion to body size.

Humans focus on objects by changing the curvature of their lens via muscles. A fish focuses by moving its lens back and forth along the line of sight (optical axis) in much the same fashion as a camera.

It's thought that at rest, fish are more or less focused on distant objects laterally (farsighted) and as a result they're a little nearsighted anteriorly (right in front of their noses). This is explained by the unique arrangement of their lens and retina, and ocular placement compared to terrestrial animals.

How fish focus has practical implications for you when presenting a fly or lure. It often works better to allow a few more feet of drift before your fly is on a fish's nose. I think it's less likely to startle them by giving them a chance to focus on your offering. (You don't want to turn that strike response into a flight response.)

RETINAS

Retinas are like the computer keyboards: the rods and cones function like keys inputting visual image information to the CPU's hard drive (brain). Information like shape, color, contrast, brightness/darkness, luminance and motion are all relayed to a fish brain, which is ready to respond with preprogrammed

The shark lens' spherical shape is similar in structure to other species of fish. See how the curved structure of the lens refracts the blue wavelengths reflected from the Sea of Cortez's azure surface.

behaviors. The dense packing of rod and cone-type photoreceptors, called mosaics, allow for the detailed discrimination of images.

When investigators reverse-engineered fish retinas, they found that some species alter their retinal hardware to adapt to

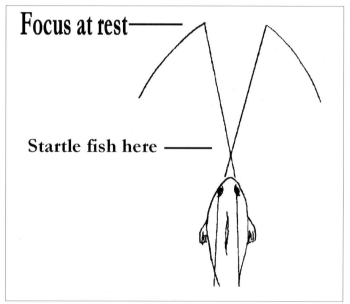

Focus at rest

Startle fish here

Fish are distantly-focused at rest. This makes them more susceptible to being startled by an imitation that's initially presented too close. Give a fish a chance to see your lure or fly in the distance, particularly in clear water.

changing aqueous environments (see sidebar "Painful Reminder" on pg. 59). For example, the ocean-dwelling salmons' retinal cones are maximally tuned to colors in the shorter end of the visible wavelength spectrum (light in the violet and blue range). This pelagic piscines' survival depends on the discernment of deep greens and blues, the primary colors of baitfish and predators in their Northwest migrations.

At homecoming, when *Oncorhynchus* noses into the estuary and heads upstream, the retinal visual pigment shifts to maximal color sensitivity in the longer wavelengths. This shift is from that of the rhodopsin (bluer seeing pigments) to the porphyropsin type, which sees the end of the spectrum that is home to the yellow, orange and reds.

Photoperiod, water temperature and hormones cue this ocular chemical change. Knowing about this color shift can help salmon and steelhead anglers pick the right lures and colors to catch their quarry! (For angling implications see sidebar "Painful Reminder" on pg. 59.)

RETINAL FINGERPRINTS

From coral reef fish to sportfish, lots of species have retinal peculiarities. Trout have retinal rod/cone mosaic arrangements that allow for UV (ultraviolet) polarized light perception. Unlike humans, it's thought that trout identify prey, manage proximity to others, determine their orientation in water and even navigate with the use of their UV polarized light retinal machinery. (See Chapters 4 and 7.)

The trout's ability to perceive polarized light takes a lot of the guesswork out of prey selection. It also presents an opportunity for the innovative angler.

HEARING

We have ears because we need them. This sounds ridiculous, but hear me out. We have external ears because sound waves don't pass very well in air. Many terrestrial animals developed these funnel-shaped devices (external ears) to catch faint, atmospheric sound waves. Fish don't need big external ears (although it's an interesting visual). They have inner ears, but lack middle and external ears because sound waves travel so much better in water—4.8 times better in fact.

Water's density makes it 14,000 times more incompressible than air. As a result, sound travels 1500 meters per second in water where it only travels 300 meters when airborne. This increased aquatic density also turns fish hearing into pressure reception. Their ability to integrate hearing and pressure sensing allows them to convert mechanoreception (sensing mechanical forces) into useful survival behaviors like finding partners, prey and avoiding predators. (Can you believe these fish, are these the only things they care about?) Over time, fish also evolved sophisticated pressure sensors and physiological transducers to differentiate between what's called near and far field sound waves.

Near and far field sound waves are aquatic noises (e.g. noisy prey vibrations) that have both particle displacement and sound pressure components.

HEAR NEAR

Near field sound exhibits particle displacement characteristics (actual physical movement), most noticeably near the source of the sound (e.g. within 8 feet for low frequencies around 100Hz). Sharks are extraordinarily sensitive to low-frequency sounds, even as low as 10Hz (undetectable to us). They're so good at this that they can hear these ultra-low frequencies from injured prey at distances up to 250 meters (good for sharks, bad for surfers).

Fish pick up these near field sounds with their inner ears and lateral line. Near field sound lives up to its definition of particle displacement because it actually moves the fish. Even though I spend most of my time above the water, I have experienced something similar to particle displacement during barbecue season.

I remember one summer, being at-one with my marinated chinook steaks on the propane barbecue grill. Noticing that the flame had gone out, I reached for the fire ignition button. Unaware of the accumulated propane in the barbecue, I attempted to light the fire.

I immediately experienced the combustion version of near-field sound. Not only were particles displaced, but also salmon steaks, utensils and guests. Fish differ in that it doesn't take quite as much propane to hear near-field particle displacement.

When a striped bass hears a nearby grasshopper plop, the impact of the prey object hitting the surface causes a water particle displacement that actually moves the fish. In the fish's inner ear (see otolith graphic) there are structures that resemble tiny fluid-filled gourds, lined on the inside by hair-like mechanoreceptors or sensing nerves. Inside this hair-lined gourd are tiny ear-stones, called otoliths.

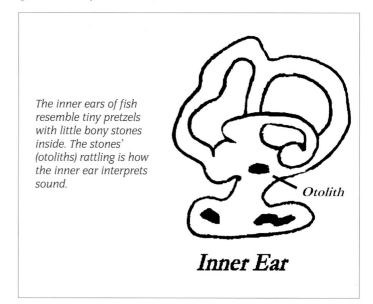

The inner ears of fish resemble tiny pretzels with little bony stones inside. The stones' (otoliths) rattling is how the inner ear interprets sound.

Otolith

Inner Ear

As a fish moves from near-field particle displacement, the otoliths rattle in the gourd like a Mexican maraca. The otoliths trigger the hair-like neurons lining the gourds, which is then interpreted as sound by the fish's brain.

As fish register and interpret these near-field sounds, some are logged as background noise and tuned out, others are called dinner.

HEAR FAR

At higher frequencies, you get what's called far field sound which has less particle displacement and results in much less whole-fish movement. Because there's less jarring, we (as fish) can't rely on the otolithic rattling alone to register sound. In this far-field component of sound, fish employ the use of the specialized structures known as airbladders. Airbladders (a.k.a. swimbladders) function as sound pressure transducers that help stimulate auditory nerves and often extend forward near the auditory bones to facilitate this.

JUST WHERE DO YOU DRAW THE LATERAL LINE?

On most fish you can readily see a line of pores running from head to tail demarcating the upper and lower scales. This network of pores contains a series of sensory structures called

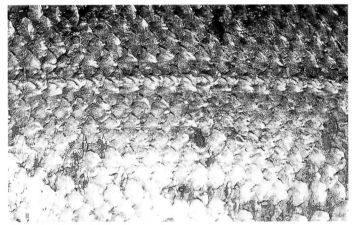

Examples of a tuna, salmon, and striped bass lateral lines. The tuna lateral line is less distinct than the others.

The salmon's lateral line is clearly demarcated.

neuromasts, which collectively comprise the lateral line (a.k.a. the acoustico-lateralis system).

Once the movement of water pressure enters the lateral (side) pores and triggers the neuromasts, neurological information is sent to the fish brain (see neuromast diagram, Chapter 5). This marvelous arrangement provides a "distant touch" for fish.

The lateral line is especially sensitive to frequencies emitted by aquatic prey. If you think about it, it just makes good sense. Evolutionarily, fish that are equipped with lateral lines get more prey and are more fit to survive. The fit ones get all the girls, and get to pass their prey-getting, lateral-line genes onto the next generation.

So guys, it pays to be like fish: sensitive and feeling.

The pore-like entrances to this striper's lateral line looks like a series of white dots. Within each pore is a network of neuromasts picking up slight water-pressure movements.

Sportfish Download

"More than ever, the creation of the ridiculous is almost impossible because of the competition it receives from reality."

— Robert A. Baker (1937-) U. S. author.

Kenny recounted his story about a little-known run of Alaskan king salmon on their murky migration up a glacial river. Ten seconds into the story, he hesitated and offered a disclaimer. He admitted that he hadn't actually seen these finned creatures himself, I suspect hoping that in trade we'd believe the guy who told him was credible. OK, I thought, this is one of those stories: Sasquatch, UFOs, Crystal angels and now this blind migration salmon story.

You see, Kenny's source was also a guide and took anglers on raft trips just like the one we were on. The story has it that they were fishing the June run of kings down from Lake Iliamna at a time when there was lots of runoff. This high water mixed with fine glacial silt and turned the river into a ribbon of gray chocolate milk.

Thirty- to 40-pound chinooks were coursing their way up to spawn, which wasn't unusual at all, except that they were supposedly "swimming with their heads up out of the water."

That's what Kenny's friend told him, "The kings swam up the river with their heads out of the water."

Hearing this, everyone in our group raised their eyebrows with that "sure they did" lie detector look on their face. Everybody except me.

It's not that I believe this story; it's ridiculous. But you might want to ask yourself, what if it did happen? Being a scientist and skeptic, I question everything, even the improbable. I mean, if those fish were doing this, what purpose could it have served? Is it possible they were looking for a sign, something to help them see where they were going?

I know this lightweight Alaskan legend reads like a *National Enquirer* headline. I can see it now; "Migratory salmon receive transmissions from outer space." What's next? How about "Salmon and tuna receive an encrypted message through a "third eye" in the center of their forehead!" Scientist says, "It's a satellite feed coming over a broadband download."

The usual suspects: (Left to right) Steve, Marty, Kenny and Bill.

Believe it or not, something like that does happen. So is it possible that the kings were receiving transmissions?

DOWNLOAD TO THE PINEAL GLAND

The pineal gland is a small glandular structure close to the brain, lying immediately beneath a translucent, optical lens-like, area of the skull. This glandular mass is innervated with neural tissue—similar to a retina, that responds to light, polarized light.

It's now theorized that salmon use their pineal glands to navigate during their ocean voyage. They do this by orienting themselves to the plane of polarized light refracted from the sun (see Chapter 4, sidebar polarized light).

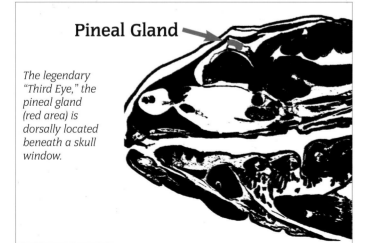

Pineal Gland

The legendary "Third Eye," the pineal gland (red area) is dorsally located beneath a skull window.

Salmonids aren't the first argonauts theorized to have used polarized light as part of their navigational guidance systems. Some scientists suspect that Vikings used refractive birefringent minerals from Iceland, called Sun Stones, (see graphic of calcite) to guide their early marine expeditions.

Whether Leif Erikson used a Sun Stone as a sextant or not, salmonids likely download polarized light to guide them.

Orienting to polarized light isn't the only ability attributed to the pineal gland. In addition to the retinal cone-like tissue I mentioned, this gland secretes melatonin (implicated in sleep cycles and jetlag) and the neurotransmitter serotonin, chemicals that both show marked diurnal changes.

Diurnal changes (i.e. twice daily) of the pineal compounds (melatonin and serotonin) are seen in salmonids. The highest concentration of each is at night. Not only are these brain chemicals influenced by the time of day but fish behavior is also.

Most anglers are familiar with a diurnal event: the early morning and late afternoon "bite." In marine environments these events correspond to the twice-daily vertical migration of baitfish and phytoplankton through the water column and the refraction of the maximum vertical component of aquatic polarized light (see Chapter 4 on light). There's lots of evidence to show these are all connected.

Polarized light may have other significant impacts on angling, marine and freshwater. For example, those morning and evening bites seem more pronounced on clear days. On the other hand, the bites on overcast days seem to last longer and are less obvious.

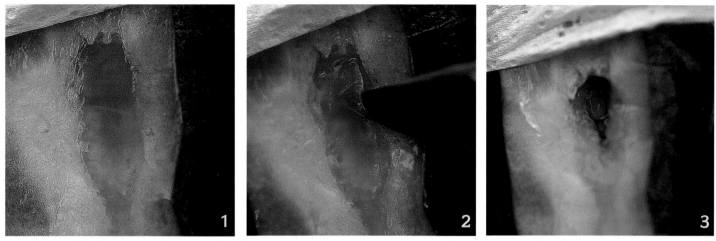

Photo 1: With the top (dorsal) aspect of the chinook's skull removed, the translucent cartilaginous "window" to the brain is clearly depicted. Photo 2: Brain surgery with a Leatherman Tool. Photo 3: This 25-pound chinook's brain is really quite small, about the size of a pinto bean. It's obvious that in the evolution of fish, nature has dictated what brain volume there is, should be dedicated to survival interests.

If there's something to this, you might want to check out the weather for future outings. If a bright sunny day is forecasted, it's more important to get out on the water early, and hang around later in the evening.

Maybe you already know this, but now you have more scientific reasoning underlying your beliefs.

Looking like a deer blinded by headlights, I landed this fly-caught chinook just as it turned dark.

Calcite (calcium carbonate) reflects polarized light well. Vikings used pieces of calcite called "Sun Stones" as sky compasses to navigate northern waters. Legend has it that Norsemen would look straight upwards towards a patch of blue sky and rotate the calcite until a blue tinge turned a yellowish hue. The direction of the yellow coloration determined the direction homeward.

Mexican pangas in the morning.

This fish was caught in the crepuscular hours of the evening. The fish's pineal gland is photosensitive, like the eye's retinal tissue, and is especially tuned to the early-morning and late-evening hours.

One benefit of fishing the evening crepuscular hours: beautiful sunsets.

How one sportfish adapts

"The world is fixed, we say: fish in the sea, birds in the air. But in the mangrove swamps by the Niger, fish climb trees and ogle uneasy naturalists who try unsuccessfully to chase them back into the water. There are things still coming ashore."

— Loren Eiseley

Evolution is a funny thing.

I don't mean ha-ha funny, I mean odd, ironic. As students of evolution, we learn that the rigors of nature exert biological pressures over generations, which favor the development of traits that facilitate an animal's survival on the planet.

Ho hum. . . get the No-Doz.

Sometimes I just don't see it.

Take my dog Buck for example.

Bucky-boy is a fine chocolate lab from professional-field-trial-and-gun-dog lineage (I'll spare you the details). Buck's genome codes for all the Labrador retriever traits that have been deemed useful by the pressures of natural selection—or at least, a good hunting-dog breeding program. As a result, Buck has quite a bit of genetic field trial potential.

His ancestors, going all the way back to the ancestral Labrador retriever, the St. John's waterdog, retrieved well, got

Genetically born to retrieve. Waterfowl, slippers or teddy bears, many generations of selective retriever breeding finds a way to express itself.

rewarded and were allowed to breed. As a result, more of Buck's ancestors were delivered by the doggy-stork, which brings us to present time where Buck is now. He's born to retrieve.

So can someone explain to me why the closest Buck gets to retrieving waterfowl, is when he proudly displays his teddy bear mounted amongst a set of sparkling white canines?

Jan says, "You've ruined that dog!"

I'd like to think he'd retrieve ducks given a chance, but in a sad way, Buck has adapted to his environment, as have we all.

Some adaptations seem to be more survival oriented than others. There are no teddy bears for sportfish, only prey to be eaten, partners to pursue. The law of the water is simple: adapt or die.

THE SURVIVORS

A couple of survivors of the sportfish evolutionary game handled environmental visual problems in two completely different ways. Salmon had to deal with their transition from a marine to freshwater environment (see Chapter 8 sidebar 1). Stripers have to deal with changing turbidity and water temperatures.

Each adaptation, whether it is compensation for salinity, turbidity or temperature, has its own angling implications. Again, this is another example of knowing the science behind the species, which in turn allows for more satisfying fishing.

Striped bass are great examples of extremely scrappy fish that adapt well to new environments. Stripers flourish on both coasts of North America, and in many freshwater bodies in-between. *Morone saxatilis* (striped bass) are successful predators in the true sense of the word. They deftly use their sensitive acoustico-lateralis (hearing/feeling) system in concert with their enhanced visual system to survive in often sub-optimal conditions.

As with all species, stripers have certain temperature requirements. Problem is, they have had to thrive in environments that didn't provide ideal temperatures. Perciformes (which includes the Centrarchids or black bass and the Moronidae which are the temperate basses like stripers) don't start getting interested in life until the temperature reaches 50 degrees, springtime in North America. You'll see them spawn around 55 to 65 degrees Fahrenheit, and the big dominant stripers like 64.4 to 68 degrees Fahrenheit best to hang with buds and feed.

In the warmer months the dominant stripers (and a lot of other species) have to find deeper water to find their preferred temperature zone (see Chapter 2 sidebar Get Edgy). Over time, this leaves the smaller stripers to tough it out in the warmer upper layers. This isn't all that bad for the smaller, less-dominant fish, because an increased body surface-area per unit weight requires warmer water to meet its metabolic needs.

One potential downside for a big fish in the cooler water below is that sometimes it doesn't contain enough oxygen for optimal visual functioning. The good news is that their eyes have adapted to deal with compromised dissolved oxygen levels.

REVIEW

In the vertebrate eye, the retina is similar to photographic film in a camera. So when waterborne light images enter the striper's anterior eye, they pass through the lens and finally converge on the retina's layer of light-sensitive rods and cones. Here

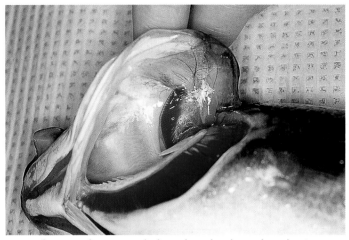

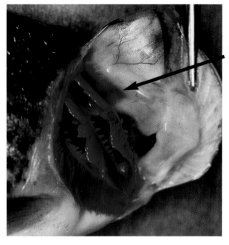

Pseudobranch

When you compare a striper pseudobranch to this trout's (barely visible), apparently size does matter in the fish-vision business.

Hopped-up muscle cars aren't the only turbo-charged mechanisms. The striper retina is supercharged with oxygen by this pseudobranch; a modified gill structure that some fish use in oxygen-compromised environments.The pseudobranch is the smaller gill-like structure rising 90 degrees perpendicular to the larger crescent-shaped gill arch.

the light image makes a mechano-chemical impression on the retinal-light and color sensitive-nerve endings (rods and cones). This imprint is then transmitted to the brain's optic lobes, where it is interpreted as an object.

THE POINT

Great system, but the retina's rods and cones are high-maintenance items, and as such require a lot of oxygen to function properly.

As noted, this can be a problem in warm water and any time that dissolved oxygen risks being depleted (e.g. dying phytoplankton or on cloudy days).

Whatever the cause, stripers visually deal with low oxygen by using an organ called a pseudobranch (pronounced: sue-do-brank, meaning "false gill").

HERE'S HOW IT WORKS

As the diagram depicts, oxygen-depleted blood returning from muscles tired from swimming, gets pumped to the gills in order to pick up a

new supply of oxygen extracted from the water (see Chapter 10—Fish Handling). Once oxygenated, the majority of blood gets pumped back to the fish's brain and body. In order to deal with the ocular oxygen demand, some blood supercharged with oxygen by the gill-like pseudobranch, gets shunted directly to the vascular beds infiltrating the high O_2 demanding retinas.

Not all species are so well equipped. Catfish don't have psuedobranchs because they don't specialize in vision. Instead, they rely on other enhanced sensory abilities—like taste buds all over their body. (Catfish in low-visibility bottom conditions "taste" their way around, feeding mostly at night.)

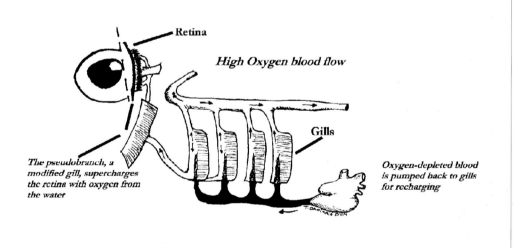

A Detroit-design-inspired schematic of the pseudobranch system.

Chapter Four

Light

"*Though it is not invariable, the pressure of natural selection is frequently of such intensity as to seem to operate not through its subtler modes but by the very threat of death, by calling forth new adaptations as the only alternative to sudden and complete extinction.*"

— *H.W. Smith*, From Fish to Philosopher, *1959*

A fish tale.

A FISH TALE

In my dream I hooked a giant fluorescent crimson and green salmon which suddenly made a tremendous downstream run into a gnarly logjam.

With a massive head jerk, the glowing giant pulled me after it into the deep watery realm of the coniferous snag. Consciousness slipping, I searched desperately for any sign of the surface. Finally, a faint whisper of light peeked around a trunk of hemlock.

Half-awake, I found myself muttering, "The light, get to the light."

I knew I was in big trouble.

I awoke to the glow of my computer monitor. Surrounded by a huge pile of research papers, a dozen fish-nerd science texts and a myriad of medical tomes, my office looked like the den of a photographic, fly tying/angling/gear-crazed fish scientist hitting bottom.

This is disgusting.

The truth is I'm in denial and I qualify for a 28-day stint in the Orlando Wilson wing of the Betty Ford Center. I can't take this anymore.

THE ADDICTIVE SUBSTANCE

For going on two years now, I have been thinking, experimenting, getting excited, drinking coffee, conspiring and investigating to see if you knew what I knew, all the while jealously guarding my discovery.

I've been trying to figure out just the right way to do this. Obsessively ruminating over the correct way to tell you, my brethren and angling contemporaries, a deep dark secret. I just have to go ahead and blurt it out.

It's all about the light.

Okay, so this might be a bigger deal to me than you, but just give me a chance to set things right.

I've underestimated the role light plays in angling. Think about it, back in the recesses of our minds, don't we all have some unanswered questions about light?

Here's one I've had: Why does it seem that sometimes when the water is dead calm, I can't get a bite, but when the wind disturbs the surface a little, it seems to stimulate the action? Here's another: why is the fishing often the best at times with the least light?

Well, by now we know there's a lot more going on with fish than previously thought. A big chunk of this knowledge pertains to light. So what's the deal with light and fish? Well, for starters, fish see things that we can't.

We can't because we don't "pack the gear."

LIGHTEN UP

To explain this, a little science background is in order. Light (e.g. sunlight) has wavelengths. Very small to huge wavelengths of light exist but the ones that we're accustomed to seeing are emitted from the sun in the 300 to 1100 nm (nanometer, i.e. really small or 10-9 meters) range. Within this group, we see the 400 to 700 nm varieties (see chart on wavelengths).

UV (ultraviolet) wavelengths are in the 200 to 400 nm end of the spectrum, which is down near the dark indigo and violet colors. We're all familiar with UV light and the effects it has on certain colors that fluoresce, but humans can't see UV wavelengths. We just see the effects it has on certain materials.

"So what's the big deal if we can't see UV light?" you ask. Well, a lot of fish do pack the retinal hardware to see it and it's a big deal to them even though we're clueless. I recently discovered what a big deal it is and the implications it has on angling.

FLUORESCENCE

We're all familiar with the use of fluorescent materials in angling (Spin N' Glows, Day-Glo orange yarns, drift gear etc.). On first consideration, we might think fluorescence works because it makes something more noticeable by glowing in the dark. That's what we see but that's not necessarily what fish see.

Imagine you're a fish while viewing the underwater world as it might appear through infrared binoculars (if this is too much of a stretch, pretend you're watching COPS and this is a nighttime bust on your neighborhood). Most of the background is monochromatic shades of gray and the subjects that create heat seem to glow green in the foreground. Well, many fish have specialized retinal "hardware" that enables them to discern UV-reflecting surfaces.

Not only can some fish see UV wavelengths but they can also see a particular characteristic of it.

They see polarized light!

Polarized light is important because it just may be the continuous thread of connection between the fish's world and our understanding of what they see. Polarized light is implicated in many facets of a fish's life. It dictates how mayflies find water, lots of insects and sea creatures use it and we know it's thought to help anadromous fish migrate.

And some fish use reflected polarized light to swim in formation with their fellow school mates (herring) and some use it to know who's good to eat and who's good to avoid.

SHADES OF POLARIZATION

"Well, mister big-shot fish doctor, what exactly is polarization?" you ask.

It all started with a guy named Edwin Land (of the Polaroid-Land camera fame). Ed had this love-hate relationship with headlight glare so he set out to find a way to combat it. He developed a material that eliminated the glare from oncoming headlights, which is a lot like the water-reflected glare that anglers deal with.

When superimposed linear polarizing filters are in parallel alignment with each other, the overlapped area allows polarized light through both because both filters' "picket fence" are oriented in the same direction.

When one filter is oriented perpendicular to the other, each "picket fence" is perpendicular to the other, which blocks out any polarized light. This creates a dark overlap because no light can get through both filters

What we interpret as unpleasant glare is mostly horizontally oriented polarized light. Polarized sunglasses incorporate a thin sheet of Ed's polarizing material which blocks out the horizontal component of reflected light (glare) but allows the vertical component of light through. The polarizing material can do this because it functions like a vertically-oriented picket fence that lets the vertical polarized light (good light) through and blocks out the horizontally polarized light (a.k.a. glare, or bad light). We can't see the pickets because they're so small.

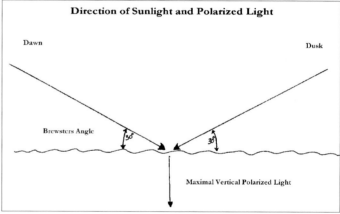

The crepuscular hours (dawn and dusk) are when the sun's light is at Brewster's angle (30 degrees). At 30 degrees, the maximal amount of vertical polarized light (this is what fish like) is transmitted (refracted) beneath the water's surface. What we interpret as glare, gets reflected off the water.

Anglers don polarized sunglasses to deal with this type of light, but what about fish? Do they care?

When sunlight contacts a fish's watery domicile, some polarized light is reflected (bounced up) upwards and some is refracted (enters the water) downwards into the water column. The time of day you get the most polarized light refracted into the water column is during the crepuscular (dawn and dusk) times of day. This is when the angle of the sun approaches what is known as Brewster's angle (approximately 30 degrees).

Fish do care about polarized light, especially when it's in the ultraviolet wavelengths. Not that they have a hard time seeing colors like blue, green, yellow and red. They see all of them,

It always seems the best fish are caught late in the day.

it's just that in their world, they use these colors to process information about motion and form. For example, if fish could talk, they might say something like, "Check out that green log coming downstream, or that guy sure has a lot of yellow crud on the bottom of his red boat. . ."

Anglers aren't really interested in what a fish thinks about logs or their gear-keeping habits but they do care how fish respond to prey because that relates to fishing. Prey detection is a whole other kettle of fish and herein lies the utility of polarized light. Polarized light helps fish, that can see it, determine what's appropriate to eat in an environment where prey discrimination can be challenging.

SEPARATING THE PREDATORS (MEN) FROM THE PREY (BOYS)

Have I mentioned that you've got to consider the aquatic environment? It's pretty variable down there. It gets murky, and goes by dietary descriptions like pea soup, coffee or tea. When water goes off color, everything looks green or shades of brown and red. Predators in this kind of environment go hungry if they can't tell the difference between a crustacean and a clump of crud. Going without a few meals is evolution's pep talk. And nature's motivational moments have spurred some fantastic adaptations.

Imagine you're a trout, seeing the polarized reflection from a baitfish's scales, a chronomid's carapace or a beetle's exoskeleton. They're all screaming "eat me." You, being a fish that can read the writing (or polarized light) on the wall, do the right thing, you devour them.

SO WHAT?

At this point if you're saying "Big deal, how will this help me get into fish," go read the sidebar on pg. 38.

I press on for those ascribing to delayed gratification.

UNDERWATER COLOR SHIFTS

If you think about it, most fish caught in moving water are hooked in depths of less than 6 feet. And most of them are caught around 3 feet of depth where they're feeding (see Chapter 2, Aquatic Environment). So the first thing to ask yourself is, "Where am I likely to find fish given their physiological requirements?"

When you get your answer, look there first.

Fish in lacustrine (lake) environments prey on baitfish, invertebrates and the occasional small rodent, but in general, color has limited usefulness the deeper you go. In a deep, green lake, a rainbow trout views a brown phantom midge (*Chaoborus* spp.) as just plain dark except for its UV light-reflecting carapace. It's not until shallower depths that color gains importance.

As the table below depicts, colors with the longest wavelengths attenuate first with increasing depth. So for perfectly clear water, reds and oranges will fade first and appear gray before yellows and greens, in that order.

Color attenuation varies with conditions like turbidity caused by particulate matter (algae, phytoplankton) or detritus (deteriorating plant materials), but the relationship of long wavelength colors diminishing first with depth, stays in effect.

A red lure below the depth that red light can penetrate will appear dark (gray) just as a yellow lure below the depth yellow light reaches, starts looking gray also. The exception to this rule is fluorescent colors. Fluorescent colors convert light of shorter wavelengths and transform it to light of slightly longer wavelengths (like invisible UV converted to visible light).

The key to lure fishing is to understand contrast. A lure has to contrast with the background it's in for the fish's retina to notice it as something out of the ordinary. When a fluorescent

Wavelengths of Light in Nanometers							
UV							IR
375	400	450		500		650	700

Colors and the light emitted from them, have specific frequencies or wavelengths that identify them.

color reflects longer wavelengths of light that's unique to the environment, it really stands out.

Most spinners and spoons work by challenging a fish's territory, resulting in a strike response. Certainly we're not trying to match a chartreuse Dardevle hatch but we are trying to get a fish's attention. And to get them to notice, they have to be able to see your lure.

SAME OLD THING

What does a fish consider ordinary? Well for starters, ordinary are the colors that predominate in the environment. The fish's retinal pigments are maximally tuned to these colors, whatever they may be. To an ocean-going tuna, shades of blue would seem pretty normal. But the ability to only see blue won't help when predators come around. A blue predator against an azure background has the tendency to become invisible. A fish has got to notice camouflaged predators as distinct from the background they're in otherwise they'll get eaten.

A fish retina functions much the way a computer does. Things are either on or off which is called the binary mode. In a fish's retina, a particular nerve cell (cone) is either on or off. If the color hitting the retina is blue (or whatever color the retinal cones are maximally tuned for) the cell is in the off position. Off translates to the predominant color of the environment, or what a fish would consider business as usual.

When something contrasts, like a different color or something more luminous shows up, the cell switches to the on position and a signal is sent to the brain. The pattern in which all these cells are arranged allows for the fish to discern contrast in a very cool way. This method of contrast discernment is called "border enhancement." Border enhancement is simply noticing differences in color and luminosity that allows a fish to see the outline of an object in nature, such as prey and predators. Ultimately, border enhancement creates contrast and when there's contrast, fish sit up and take notice.

Water colored by particulate matter; muddy, silty, turbidwater, presents a "particular" problem. If the water we're fishing is green, it's that wavelength because the particulate matter in the water is absorbing all the colors with shorter wavelengths up to the predominate shade in the water (green). Consider using lures with longer wavelengths than the predominant staining color of the water and use fluorescent colors if you especially want the color to show up.

Some have criticized certain color use in particular waters because they say the color just turns black. Well, maybe that's not all bad when you know how a fish retina works.

Angling tip: The take-home lesson for anglers is to think contrast. No wonder black works so well.

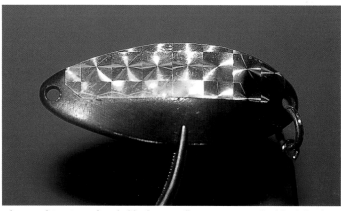

The combination of scale-like brass reflective tape and a black background provides contrast no matter what the water conditions.

UV, Phosphorescence, Fluorescence

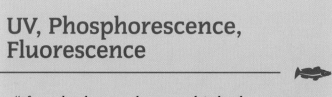

"If anybody says he can think about quantum problems (physics) without getting giddy, that only shows he has not understood the first thing about them."

— *Niels Henrik David Bohr (1885-1962)*
Danish physicist.

Niels was a tight-ass in the lab, but streamside, he was a Danish party animal; and you know what that means......Tuborgs and Atlantic salmon!

Physics and drift fishing were two things that got Neils' electrons orbiting, and he saw that quantum mechanics had the potential to get into some of those hook-nosed Atlantics just outside of town!

Molecular physics? Fishing?

Quantum mechanics explains how electrons behave under certain circumstances, for example, light hitting fluorescent colors. Fluorescent colors (the paints, pigments etc.) glow because they emit light. . . this attracts fish.

Fluorescence is basically light-absorbing fluorochromes (pigments) emitting light at a slightly longer wavelength than initially illuminated them (review from Chapter 4).

For example, if you take a fluorescent material and charge it with light energy (from the sun or a flashlight, etc.), the atoms in the fluorochrome pigment get all excited, like boiling water. It's as if they're rising to the next orbital floor on the electron elevator. A fraction of a second later (actually 10^{-8} seconds), the elevated electrons relax and drop back to their original level. As they descend, a photon or packet of light, with a slightly longer wavelength than the original light shown on it, gets ejected. Voila—the appearance of glow!

As in the photo, the fluorochrome pigments in the threads will fluoresce, or emit longer, visible wavelengths when exposed to UV light (shorter, invisible to humans unaided). When I turn my blacklight (UV) off, these fluorescent colors quit glowing and can't be seen. (I tried to take a picture of this, but was reminded why we can't see much without light.)

When you get these materials out of the lab and into the water, these types of fluorescent colors work well as fish attractors in low-light periods, especially during the crepuscular times

Illuminated with ultraviolet light, these white plastic spools of fluorescent threads emit light (photons) at a slightly longer wavelength than the UV illumination.

of day. You'll often see fluorescent materials incorporated in the head and tail wraps of flies and on lures and spinners. Their light-emitting characteristics are the reason for their success.

From the fish's visual context, fluorescent materials provide contrast (light emitted where there is little) and that's what matters to fish.

The specific color a fluorochrome emits depends on its spectra. But basically there are all types of fluorescent colors with differing brightness. Each fluorochrome requires a certain incident (incoming) light wavelength and will emit its own longer wavelength color as a result.

FLUORESCENCE AND WATER COLOR

Each body of water has its characteristic color too (clear blue, green with phytoplankton, tannin-stained brownish-red). If the river seems primarily green, it's because the particulates in the water absorb most of the other shorter wavelengths so all you see is green. Same goes for other colors. The key here is to remember the wavelength spectra is a one-way street for fluorescence.

PRACTICAL APPLICATION IN CLEAR-TINTED WATERS

Because fluorescent colors always emit light at a longer wavelength than they were exposed to, you need to use a fluorescent color up the spectra (longer wavelength) from the predominant water color, if you want it to be most visible. For example, in clear green water, fluorescent blue won't work well because the plant life in the water sucks up the entire blue wavelength light so there's not much blue available. Go up the spectrum (longer wavelength) from your background color and use fluorescent yellow. In tannin-stained water, which is farther up the spectrum from the green water, use a fluorescent correspondingly up the spectrum too, like orange or red.

Angling tip: go to a camera store or underwater videography supply outlet and buy colored filters that match the water colors you'll likely encounter (green, brown, tan etc.). View your lures and flies through these filters to see if they produce contrast.

Whatever provides the most contrast, especially with lures that elicit a protective or territorial response, is the best way to go.

PHOSPHORESCENCE

Some materials continue to glow even in the absence of external light (much like Chernobyl). You've seen this with those glow sticks you break that emit green light. The light emission is a temperature-dependant event called phosphorescence (i.e. the glow-in-the-dark phenomenon). Glow-in-the-dark (phosphorescent) colors have phosphors that, once illuminated, continue to emit light even in the absence of any other source. Their electrons just can't relax once exited, like fluorescent colors do.

This reminds me of a story.

My first angling experience with phosphorescence was while fishing Lake Taupo in New Zealand. My kiwi guide swore me to secrecy, but since there's no New Zealand angling statute of limitations, who's gonna know?

Fly-fishing Lake Taupo, at the drainage of the Tongariro River, in total darkness seemed weird to me. The only way I was able to rationalize this 4 a.m. snipe hunt was by accomplishing one of the two things I really wanted to do while in the Southern Hemisphere: I wanted to observe the Southern Cross constellation (check that one off, done). The other one was to see which

way toilet water spiraled when flushed (bad news: it doesn't flush any different in New Zealand than here). Now, after having looked at the stars, I'm figuring this morning's activity to be a $200 boat ride.

I figured my guide was just going through the motions, until he pursed his lips and apprehended his lit flashlight from a chest pocket, he reminded me of a giraffe picking fruit from a prickly branch. Then he reached for his fly wallet and pulled out a rather sparse leechy-looking pattern and started wrapping phosphorescent tape around the body. After cloaking the fly, he "charged" it with the lip-bound pocket flashlight and issued terse instructions. I was told to take my rod loaded with a sinking shooting head, cast the fly, wait for it to settle on the bottom and then start a slow retrieve.

A beautiful 7-pound rainbow, now on the wall downstairs, was apparently a phosphor-o-phile (lover of all that glows) because it wasn't three pulls and it was drag-setting time. Hoping for a highly technical explanation, I asked our guide why this light-charged fly worked. "Because they can see it", he replied.

He shoots, he scores. . . Kiwi Guide: 1, Fish Doctor: 0.

What happened: The flashlight delivered a light-wavelength cocktail causing the benthic bug to glow. The radioactive leech looked good to the rainbow, so he took it. Eerily shimmering prey items aren't unusual for sportfish; they're actually common. This was an innovative angler taking advantage of a biological precedence in nature: bioluminescence or glow-in-the-dark creatures.

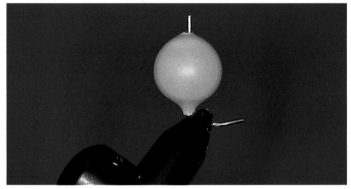

Phosphors (materials that continue to emit light) are interesting to fish. Lots of prey items glow in the dark (bioluminescence) so aquatic predators take notice of things that generate light in a contrasting dark environment.

Wristwatch numerals, light sticks and this walk-meter face, all incorporate phosphorescent materials, which work on the principle of continuous emission of light.

Fluorocarbon Technology

"There are many examples of old, incorrect theories that stubbornly persisted, sustained only by the prestige of foolish but well-connected scientists. . . Many of these theories have been killed off only when some decisive experiment exposed their incorrectness. . . Thus the yeoman work in any science, and especially physics, is done by the experimentalist, who must keep the theoreticians honest."

Michio Kaku, Hyperspace, *Oxford University Press, 1995, p 263. (1)*

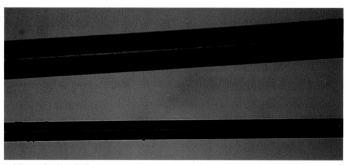

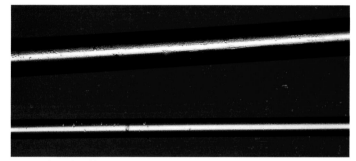

Although the difference in diameters of the nylon (top) and fluorocarbon (bottom) is mostly due to pound-strength ratings, these photomicrographs (photos taken through a microscope) show the differences in polarized light reflectivity when viewed under linear polarized filters in parallel.

Even when the filters are perpendicular (i.e. crossed polars), reflected polarized light comes through because of the leader's characteristic of birefringence. Birefringence is a measure of a material's ability to bend polarized light 90 degrees, thereby allowing it to get through the second, perpendicularly oriented, filter. Some of the basic research with fluorocarbon was done with polarized light illumination to determine its refractive index.

When I first started looking into the fluoro-carbon monofilament issue, I smugly assumed it was just another marketing hype-job. The line doesn't look all that different on first glance. The manufacturer's claims for fluoro-carbon materials are bold. Supposedly, fluoro-carbon lines are less visible in water than nylon, sink faster, take abrasion better and are more impervious to chemicals. I was expecting them to say that if you flossed with it, you'd raise your IQ.

A skeptic by training and previous gear purchases, I launched into a forensic gear investigation. The first thing I did was "borrow" a 2-foot sample of fluoro-carbon tippet from my buddy Seth. He shot me one of those, "Okay man, but only if you have to" looks. I figured I had to because I didn't have any and he did. It would be a while before I got to town, and I already knew it was really expensive. I took a sample of my own nylon leader (I'm not that cheap), placed the samples side by side on my Olympus microscope and summarily spun the 10X objective into position like a gunslinger checking his six-shooter for bullets.

I was wrong.

The fluoro-carbon looks *better* than the nylon. I wasn't expecting any difference.

To make sure I was correct about being wrong, I viewed the fluoro-carbon and nylon monofilament in both regular microscopic illumination and under polarized light.

The fluoro-carbon material is clearer and extruded more smoothly than nylon. (Extrusion is the process where a material is forced out of a die to form the line.) Since the surface is a lot smoother, there are fewer reflective surfaces from the fluoro-carbon than nylon surfaces. Rough surfaces create more reflection.

The ads say the refractive index of fluoro-carbon is better than nylon. To bring perspective, the refractive index (r.i.) of water is around 1.33 for water, 1.35 for fluoro-carbon and 1.53 for nylon. This puts fluoro-carbon closer to water compared to nylon, making it appear "more invisible" once immersed. Additionally, fluoro-carbon lines weigh about 50 percent more than nylon. Because of this, they sink faster: water weighs 1 gram per cc (1 cc is equal to a milliliter or a cubic centimeter...about a quarter-inch cube), nylon weighs 1.21 grams per cc and fluorocarbon weighs approximately 1.77 grams per cc.

COULD SOMETHING BE GOING ON HERE?

I think there might be a few reasons why fluorocarbon catches more fish than nylon. It might be that because it's stiffer it might make the fly or lure behave differently. Personally, I think this is the least likely. Another possibility lies in the specific gravity.

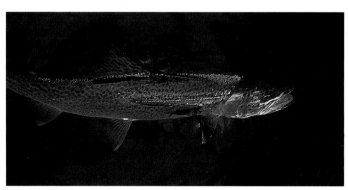

If you look closely, you can see the glare from the nylon leader.

Fluoro-carbons get you down to where the fish are quicker. I think there's a good chance this helps a lot. But there's another factor that personally speaks to me: the refractive index.

Obviously, if a fluoro-carbon tippet is clearer, it's less visible to fish. When you look at the two materials in water side by side, they're both pretty invisible (see graphic). Given water's turbidity and fish not having the visual acuity we do, I don't think the issue is whether the line is visible in the water or not. I think the issue is how the visibility appears in a fish's context. Neither type of material casts a significant silhouette but they do both reflect light and fluoro-carbon reflects less polarized light than nylon.

I suspect polarized light reflection from leaders, lines and tippets have been spooking fish. Experienced anglers will take a little fine mud or silt and gently rub the last few feet of their leader, just enough to cut the sheen of the material. Some say to make it sink (break the surface tension) but maybe it helps cut the reflection also.

The polarized light theory as a means of prey enhancement should work for you and not against you. You want your prey imitation to reflect polarized light, not your leader.

Here's a question for scientific anglers: If fluoro-carbon lines catch more fish, does cloud cover or amount of sunlight, effect the catch rate when you're using it? This would be good information that could be gleaned from our angling journals.

FIELD TRIAL

How do I like using fluoro-carbon "in the field"? Actually, I don't like it. It makes weird sounds with fish on. I tested 20-pound-test

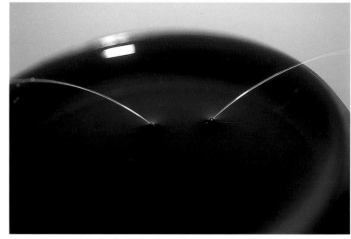

Nylon on the left, fluorocarbon on the right, the nylon is barely more visible to the human eye under water.

fluoro-carbon line, while drift fishing for chinook in Alaska. When a big fish was on (big to me equals more than 20 pounds, poor me), the line groaned and squealed like an alien in estrus. I kept thinking my line was going to break.

It's also harder to tie knots with fluoro-carbon. Something about it heating up and breaking when you snug 'em down. I guess I could get used to it, but I like nylon better.

Now if the fishing is tough and I've got leader-shy fish, I won't hesitate to use fluoro tippets for flies or run some off a swivel. But I'm sticking with nylon for my level wind.

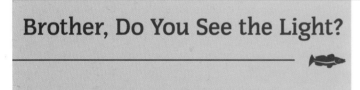

Brother, Do You See the Light?

"We see only what we know."

Johann Wolfgang von Goethe (1749-1832)
German poet, dramatist

Come on, we all know some angling materials work better than others. And in fly-fishing, everyone has their preference.

It's possible that we just like the way one material looks more than another does, so we use it more. We catch some fish with it and we (erroneously) attribute our angling success to the material.

But what if there really is a difference in materials, which to us seem identical. Same color, size, everything. But could some materials reflect light differently than others? What if the real prey in nature reflects light differently from our imitations, only we can't see the difference?

Many fish prey items—insects, crustaceans, zooplankton and baitfish—reflect polarized light. Just as fish have adapted to discern polarized light in a way that helps them function in the aquatic world (via target enhancement), so I predict anglers of the future will use a knowledge of polarized light to aid in mimicking nature and deceiving their quarry.

ESKIMO MATERIALS

I've always heard polar bear hair works better than bucktail. In the past, polar bear hair was thought (erroneously) to transmit polarized light down to the bear's skin to supply heat. Laboratory research disproved this theory.

Angling results supported the idea that polar bear hair seemed to work better than other types of fur but we didn't know why for sure. Some attributed the difference to the arctic animal's coat movement in water. In my experience with buck-tailing (trolling streamer-type flies behind a boat) for coho in estuaries, the polar bear bucktails worked much better than

Mother Nature's jewelry.

deer-hair bucktails. The only difference was the origin of the fur.

Was it just that the polar bear hair moved better in water than the deer hair?

If so, with this theory, synthetics that are more supple should work better, right? Doesn't turn out that way. I've tried synthetics that move even more fluidly, but some don't produce as well as polar bear pelage.

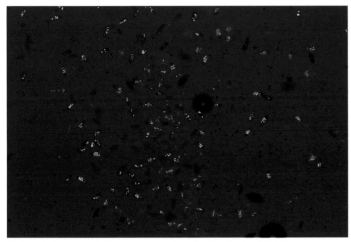

Brine shrimp exoskeleton remnants reflect polarized light, as seen here in the digestive tracts of the marine organisms that ate them. Brine shrimp and other crustaceans reflect polarized light.

While reviewing the polar bear hair literature, I came across a theory (a false one) that posited that polar bear hair evolved as a means to convert sunlight energy into conductive heat for the arctic creature. The notion that it might also be a sort of polarized fiberoptic cable piqued my interest too.

OK, maybe polarized light didn't travel down the hair, but what if it reflects polarized light better?

Well, it seems to do just that (see middle insert). Is this why it works better? Maybe. We could design an experiment to definitively test this, but there's not enough time and too many fish to catch, not to mention too little funding for it. But there's a body of evidence, albeit circumstantial, that makes the idea plausible and worthwhile investigating.

Angling to stay out of jail tip: It's illegal to have polar bear in the U.S. but you can obtain it from Canadian fly shops.

MATCHING THE HATCH, INCLUDING LUMINESCENCE

A lot has been said and done regarding insects and fish. Most freshwater fish that are currently stalked by anglers have insects as a predominant part of their diet. Fly-fishing originated from this relationship. As a result, all types of insects, from mayflies to terrestrials (beetles, ants etc.), have been imitated to entice rising trout.

It's always fascinated me that we can catch a fish with a fake. This is similar to you or I taking a big bite of a fur-and-feather Big Mac. Fish not having the visual acuity that we do goes a long way to explain the phenomenon. But I guess what fish don't have in visual acuity they make up for in knowing what to expect (conditioning).

It's surprising how many insects are conditioned by or reflect polarized light themselves. As has been stated ad nauseum, many fish see polarized light as a means to distinguish prey. For years (like close to 200) anglers have known that to match, the hatch they had to be concerned with imitating an insects size, shape, color and behavior. In light of the past few years' scientific discoveries, I say we need to complete the criteria: size, shape, color, behavior and *luminescence* (see Chapter 7).

OTHER MATERIALS

What about other angling materials? Might they have unique light-reflecting qualities?

Once I started examining materials with different polarized light reflectivity, I started cruising all the tackle and fly shops like a muskellunge looking for tender young waterfowl. I focused on reflective materials, especially the ones that imitated the guanine reflection of a fish scale. I interviewed anglers, asking which materials they thought worked best, thinking there might be a correlation between the amount of polarized light reflectivity and effectiveness.

IT'S OK TO DO THIS EXPERIMENT AT HOME, KIDS

None of this stuff is rocket science as I'm sure you've figured out by now. I've come up with a way that a sufficiently motivated angler can get a rough assessment of the relative polarized light reflectivity a material has. It's a measure of the polarization contrast.

Flashlight with a linear polarizing filter vinyl-taped in position.

Here's what you do. Go to your local camera store and get a linear polarizing filter. Now make certain that it's a linear polarizer and not a circular one. The way you can tell is by going outside and looking through the filter and rotating it. If the overall picture you see through the filter gets darker at one point and gets lighter when you rotate the filter through another 90 degrees, it's a linear filter. Take the filter and tape it to a flashlight as depicted in the photo above. Grab your polarized (required) sunglasses, take your filtered flashlight and find a dark place to view your materials or lures (you'll have some explaining to do to your friends).

Once your eyes accommodate to the dark, pin your materials on the wall, put on a Roy Orbison CD and don your shades. Illuminate your materials with the filtered flashlight while rotating the flashlight itself around its long axis. If you have a responsive material, you'll notice the material will change in reflectivity at

90-degree positions. Then remove your sunglasses, and do the same thing. There won't be any difference in reflectivity as you rotate the light without your sunglasses on. This is because the vertical orientation of the polarizing filter in your sunglasses blocks out the horizontal component of the polarized light. When you aren't wearing sunglasses you don't block anything out, so it looks the same regardless of the flashlight's orientation.

What we're looking for here are the biggest changes in brightness or luminosity (a.k.a. maximal polarization contrast). Lots of marine animals use polarization contrast to identify prey items.

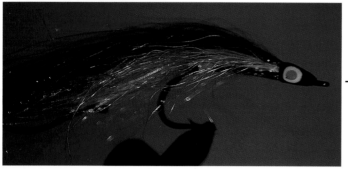

Bucktail pol = This polar bear hair bucktail fly #1, is illuminated with a representation of high-contrast polarized light.

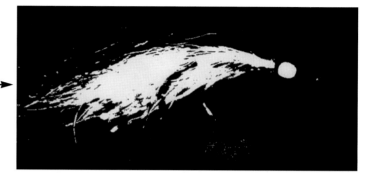

Luminosity = The same fly is measured in overall luminosity.

Bucktail pol + Bucktail fly #1, now illuminated with low-contrast polarized light. The image is darker because of the decrease in polarized light.

Lumiosity + The decrease in luminosity of bucktail #2 is quantified by its respective luminosity measurement.

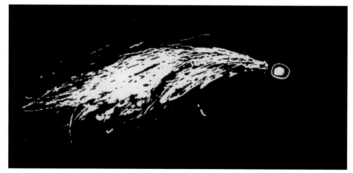

Luminosity Net: Many aquatic creatures determine their prey by polarization contrast. Represented here is the net polarization contrast (the polarization difference between luminosity = and luminosity +). The net polarization contrast imitates a prey's polarized light-reflecting capabilities.

Shedding a little light on the subject...

We're joining them.

"Seeing as how luminosity and polarized light has been such a big deal so far how about a few examples?" Well, since you ask, I guess I'll oblige.

In the sidebar on pg. 38, we came up with a way to illustrate polarization contrast. Since you and I don't see polarized light, except as glare, I figured I'd demonstrate the difference in polarization luminosity. In the graphic, one of the polar bear bucktails appears brighter. The increase in luminosity is due to high-contrast polarized light (drives fish wild). We'll call this one POL=. The bucktail image that's darker (POL+) is dimmed because of the low-contrast polarized light. You and I can obviously tell one is brighter than the other, but what a trout cares about is the net difference between the two.

If we could see what trout see, what might that difference look like?

The black-and-white graphics are exact representations of Bucktail POL= and Bucktail POL+ and I named them Luminosity = and Luminosity +, respectively. What we're interested in is the difference between the two, or the net luminosity. This is because the bigger the net luminosity, the more it will grab the attention of a sea creature that's into polarization contrast.

The graphic called luminosity net is just that, the net con-trast in terms of the luminosity that resulted from illuminating the bucktail with and without vertical polarized light (a.k.a. polarization contrast).

Another term you'll see used in this middle insert is birefringence. This is where a material will actually bend the reflected, linear polarized, light 90-degrees. The effect of this is when viewed under crossed polars, you get the 90-degree bent light coming through the overlying perpendicularly oriented filter's "picket fence", when you'd normally expect no light to come through. Some plastics are highly birefringent, as well as naturally occurring substances such as calcite (calcium carbonate) and some keratinized (skin) materials.

CONTRAST AND COMPARE

We know some angling materials contrast more in luminosity than others do. The following graphics are just a few examples. A scientific angler, with sufficient interest and time, could set up clinical trials to see if luminosity correlates with effectiveness.

Fish skin = *Plastic materials are often incorporated into lures and flies. The manufacturers of this material claim it reflects gamefish-attracting UV light in the lower wavelengths.*

Material 1= *This material exhibits a marked degree of polarization contrast. From non-scientific anecdotal reports, it's reported to be an effective fish-catching material. (high polarization contrast equates to fish catching?)*

Fish skin + *In this example, notice the purplish glow near the lower, right-hand corner of the green plastic. I suspect this is a light reflection near the UV range. Many oceangoing fish have evolved to visually key in on UV reflections.*

Material 1+ *The same material under low-polarized illumination.*

Silver Thorn = *A popular British Columbia fly, the Silver Thorn, really shows a nice polarization contrast.*

Silver Thorn + *Silver Thorn with low contrast.*

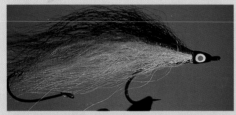

Olive Bucktail = *One of my favorite coho flies, this Olive Bucktail made with polar bear hair, has what I would term moderate contrast, but combines key features of luminosity and countershading.*

Olive Bucktail + *Olive Bucktail under low contrast.*

Squid = *My friend, Shaun Bennet, gave me this fly to evaluate. Imitating a squid pattern, the luminosity mimics the real thing in nature. Cephalopods (squids and octopus belong in this group) are well known in scientific circles for reflecting similar light-reflecting qualities.*

Squid + *Same fly, less polarized light.*

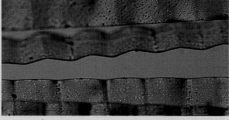

Bait scale = *This material, made to imitate bait scales, is pretty boring fully illuminated.*

Bait scale + *When viewed under crossed polars, this material is highly birefringent like many other good fish-catching materials.*

Antron = *Antron is a popular synthetic fly-tying material. Good contrast.*

Antron + *Remember, lots of fish see color.*

Fish scale + *A salmonid scale viewed under high-powered microscopy exhibits familiar polarized reflections.*

Scale tape = *It takes a while to recognize promising materials but once you get the hang of it, the results are consistent with fish catching. This tape has nice overall contrast but you really don't get the impact of its reflective qualities until viewed under higher power.*

Scale tape + *Same tape, less polarized illumination.*

Scale tape 10xmag *The same tape seen at a 10X higher magnification when viewed with polarization contrast, reminiscent of stained glass.*

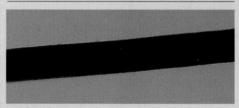

Buck tail = *Traditional buck's tail from a deer (not to be confused with a Bucktail fly made with polar bear hair or other materials) is pretty boring from a refractive perspective.*

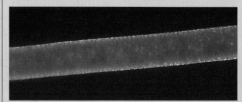

Bucktail + *I'm of the opinion that the clinical fishing results match these lackluster images compared to other high-polarization contrast materials.*

Peacock = *When wrapped on a fly, peacock herl really shows polarization contrast.*

Peacock + *Peacock herl under low polarized light.*

Polar bear = *Polar bear hair with high polarization contrast under high magnification.*

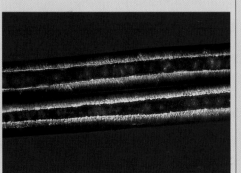

Polar bear + *with colors Polarization contrast translates to luminosity and this example of polar bear luminosity comes in brilliant, fish-attention-grabbing colors.*

Polar bear + *This polar bear hair under magnification appears more like jewelry than keratinized (skin, hair etc.) tissue.*

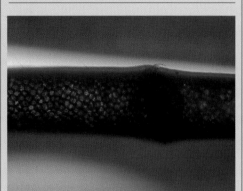

10X bucktail = *A high-magnification deer hair.*

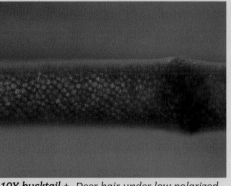

10X bucktail + *Deer hair under low polarized light.*

Polar bear 10X high mag close up. *A high-magnification look at the surface of a polar bear hair. Notice the iridescent shimmer to the refractive keratin scales.*

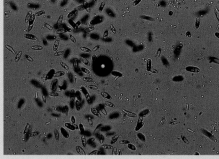

Microorgs = *Microscopic marine organisms that have eaten polarized light-reflecting crustacean exoskeletons (brine shrimp). Viewed under full illumination.*

Microorgs + *Same view and group of organisms, this time under crossed polars, showing the birefringence of the crustaceans' shell.*

Calcite = *Fragments of calcite (calcium carbonate) under polarized light.*

Calcite + *Fragments of calcite (calcium carbonate) showing birefringence. If the Viking legend of the navigational properties of calcite, or sunstone, are valid, I suspect the basis of it lies in its polarized light-bending qualities.*

Chapter Five

Sensing

"*When a tree falls in the forest and there is no one around, does it make a noise?*"

Zen koan

Though hard to see in this photo, there's a shrimp fly that hooked this snapper external to its mouth. It had a little crustacean scent attractant applied to it.

Fifteen years ago, while fishing in Campbell River, British Columbia, the self-proclaimed salmon capital of the world, I engaged the services of a guide named Mike who taught me some of the finer aspects of spring (chinook) salmon fishing. That morning, Mike and I decided to mooch (basically still-fishing) with a two- or three-ounce weight and live herring.

We started out drifting along a granite sheer-face in one of those Inside Passage whirlpools. Every so often, I'd get a hit, but every time I lifted the rod, no takers. As a last resort, I tried setting the hook quickly, which in that GPS coordinate is considered taboo.

Fish on! (But not fair-hooked.)

When I winched this salmonid slab to the surface, I saw that I'd head-snagged it. At the time, I figured the fish had first mouthed the herring and spit it out, just about the time I yanked.

When I reflect on that now, I contemplate another possibility: I think the springer was rubbing against my bait, like a cat that swipes its face on your pant's leg. (Cats do this to mark their territory with glandular cheek and chin secretions.) My salmon, however, had another motive I suspect; it wanted to taste without totally committing. Good survival behavior?

Yes.

Consider this phenomona from an evolutionary point of view. If a fish had to bite every food-sized morsel that came along in order to determine food/not food, it wouldn't survive long. One poisonous sculpin appetizer and it's all over. But if you (as fish again) could develop a way to taste something without putting it into your mouth, you'd decrease your exposure to risk.

Most of a salmonid's taste buds are on its tongue and surrounding mouth areas (buccal cavity, and there are a few more lining the esophagous). But salmonids also have taste buds on the surface of their head (and so do bass for that matter). This means they can literally taste an object just by touching it.

Some fish have taste buds all over their body. Take catfish for example: blind as bats, they taste their way around the bottom. This gustatory ability compensates for poor vision, and explains why smelly catfish bait works so well.

Fish nostrils often have olfactory pits, which are depressions lined with sensory tissue that pick up minute amounts of waterborne chemicals. Like most fish, this chinook's nostrils (or nares) are highly sensitive to amino acids (proteins).

But what are the angling implications of all this?

Well first of all, knowing that a species depends on taste makes a difference. It's also helpful to understand that taste buds are highly sensitive to phospholipids (fats or oils), like those found in many attractants and scents.

THAT SOMETHING SPECIAL: PHEROMONES

What are pheromones? Pheromones are mysterious substances secreted by animals, which chemically communicate with other animals. Though they occasionally prompt cross-species interactions, most pheromones are reproductively species-oriented.

Not all say, "come hither"; some suggest "get lost."

Fish receive chemical communications a couple of ways. Not only do they taste the messages (tastebuds) but they smell them too (olfactory tissue).

Some fish attractants contain sex hormones (pheromones) and others use whole ground-up fish products. Combinations of both these are often the most effective. There are also products specifically designed to remove scents from your hands.

A salmon can communicate chemically with amino acids in their mucus coat which in combination functions as a means of individual and sexual recognition.

Whether they know it or not, anglers talk to fish chemically, though presumably not in a language of romance. Offensive compounds such as fuels, nicotine and some proteins can really put fish off. (Given this fact, I'm hard pressed to explain why the guy who has the leakiest outboard, chain smokes and probably has lots of fish-foul smells all over his hands is often catching the biggest fish, but he must be doing something right.)

In fact, there are some compounds that will scare a fish faster than you can say L-serine—an amino acid (l-serine: a big fish offender). Researchers have found that if a steelhead picks up even minute amounts of this stuff, it will bolt out of the area.

And that's a smart move, from an evolutionary point of view. Marine mammals (seals, sea lions, killer whales), all salmonid natural predators, secrete l-serine.

So here's the angling tip: Wash your hands.

By the time you get to the water, from home, you have come in contact with petroleum products and all sorts of other compounds. Washing your hands with non-scented soap will help remove these. I'd also pass on the aftershave that day, {though you probably ought to stick with the deodorant if you're fishing with friends).

SCARY STUFF

What terrifies one fish is another's delight. The teaser fish in the photo releases oils and fluids that act as an effective chemical attractant to schooling roosterfish. While roosters offer a good example of an auditory-perceptive predator, they also appreciate the bouquet of scombroid baitfish (tuna-like).

Teaser fish do just that: tease. Teaser fish are used for their olfactory (smell) fish-attracting attributes. Once sportfish are drawn in to the vicinity by the teaser, the imitation (the fly placed below our teaser) is cast and then retrieved quickly to stimulate a strike.

Many fish, when injured, secrete skin compounds called alarm cell scents, also known as Schreckstoff substance (see histology slide at top of pg. 48).

Some alarm cell substances only mean something to members of the species that emits them, but a few predators have broken the code, developing the ability to smell or taste alarm compounds secreted by their prey. Like a prizefighter sensing an opponent's ready to go down, predatory fish often close in for the kill when they smell their prey's Schreckstoff signal.

Attractant manufacturers use baitfish alarm cell substances in their cocktails. For example, they know herring release fear compounds when attacked by salmon. In herring lingo, these fear compounds tell the herring to coalesce into balls and display all sorts of predator-confusing behaviors. In salmon lingo, the same scent spells "lunch!"

ETHICAL QUESTIONS

I've often wondered about flyfishing traditions surrounding the ethics of imitation. They seem to go something like this. It's fine to imitate the visual characteristics of the target species prey. And perhaps you can include a little auditory or lateral line stimulation, as with popper fishing. But if the auditory stimulus isn't manufactured from natural materials (excluding synthetic imitation of natural materials, go figure) you're getting on thin ice. But when it comes to selling your fly by smell, appealing to the olfactory lobes. . . we're talking a felony.

Who makes up these rules anyway?

I don't think anyone will admit to it. You're more likely to get an immediate soul-cleansing confession from a group of 7-year-olds standing around a fresh grape-drink-stained carpet. Even the slightest scientific observation dashes the entire conversation of proper fly etiquette to dust. I propose a rational direction.

Match the scent.

EAU DE HOOKUP

You heard me right. We could really get into this. Using just any old smell would be considered crude. Insects have alarm cell substances, so let's match 'em. By now you've sensed that I'm a baitfish fan, so let's match that too.

A little threadfin shad juice please.

Hey Steve, can I borrow a couple of drops of Stonefly Obsession?

The marketing opportunities are mind-boggling. We'll have more spigots than the local watering hole. I see it now, "Drives Trout Wild", "Muskie Madness", oh this is too good. Fishing for the truly deranged.

I could see myself being a bouquet devotee, but I've been told I'm alone in this. I suspect I have kindred spirits out there (maybe totaling about 20). How would I find you?

Does your spouse respond to the mention of angling with something like, "You should talk to my husband, he's really into fishing." If so, you're not into this enough.

No, the way I know you're afflicted as one who would join me in matching scents, is if your spouse breaks into uncontrollable sobbing at the mention of angling, then yessir, you're my kind of people.

Good Vibrations

"Anyone can look for history in a museum. The creative explorer looks for history in a hardware store."

— Robert Wieder

How would we have evolved differently if we grew up in the thick underwater atmosphere? Certainly our skin and nervous supply would be altered. We'd have skin sensors detecting motion. And, we'd have lateral lines. Of everything piscine, it's lateral lines I covet the most.

How lucky to be a lunker bass, hanging suspended in a green water column, canopied by dense aquatic plants. It's so dark your daytime visual guidance system is on standby, you're operating on full, holographic lateral-line-driven, hydrodynamic night-vision image generation. Fins extended, nostrils flared... You're a bad bass and you know it.

Radar indicates a target; it could be prey, maybe predator.

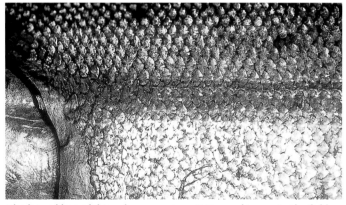

The lateral line of this salmon carries a 3-D sound image to the fish's neurological system. Notice how the lateral line continues up towards the head of the fish and inwards to where you'd expect any other animal's "ears" to be. The lateral line can be considered an evolutionary extension to a fish's "hearing."

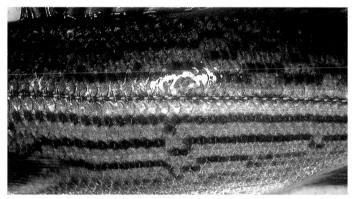

This striped bass's lateral line looks like a series of white pores. Embedded in these pores are structures called neuromasts; little tiny whisk broom-like appendages, that interpret pressure as 3-D information.

Visual doesn't read it yet, olfactory doesn't smell it, but gustatory's getting ready to taste it. Lateral line's picking up the picture, neuro from the near-field sensing forms the 3-D replication of the intruder. We've got an ID. . . It's a vibrating, 4-centimeter carapace-clicking, crustacean cloud-image coming up broadside. . . a crayfish.

You do what you're trained to do, what you're hardwired to do. You eat it. And it's good.

SOUNDS TOO GOOD TO BE TRUE

The process by which this animal moved toward the mechanical stimulus is called thigmotaxis, and the organ that detects thigmotaxic movement in fish is the lateral line.

What's a lateral line?

In Chapter 3 we mentioned how the lateral line system (lls) augments hearing but can knowledge of the lls help us catch fish?

Yes.

The lateral line system (lls) is a series of interconnected neurological receptors (neuromasts) embedded in pores along that line you see on the flanks of fish. In many sportfish, these neuromasts continue onto the surface of their head, embedded in the hard tissue that covers their bony skulls. Hidden deep in the recesses of the pores, they look like tiny whiskbrooms with exposed bristles. As incoming prey moves through the aqueous environment, the water density creates a prey-shaped sound-replica, an incoming holographic soundwave or acoustic image, which bends a neurologically interpreted image into the hair-like projectiles. It's rather like the impact of sound on your ear; like

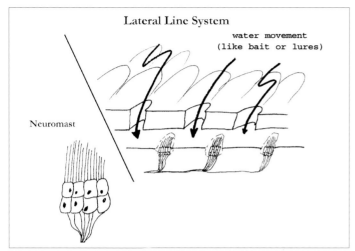

Lateral Line System

water movement
(like bait or lures)

Neuromast

As water pressure enters the pores along the lateral line, it impacts the neuromasts, which signal water movement with their hair-like projections.

This bass fly is similar to bass lures used with spinning gear. It's designed with the same objective, creating water disturbances to stimulate bass to strike.

your ear; the mechanical motion is then relayed to the bass' brain, suggesting information as vital as "eat this," or "swim for your life."

Anglers overlook the lateral line. The bass folk are quick to consider sight and taste, but the lateral-line system holds real opportunity for the hardware-inspired angler. Research shows that you can get a fish to react automatically and instantaneously to certain pressure (sound) frequencies.

When it comes to vibes, human hearing allows us to pick up sound waves around 30 Hz and upward. The fish-reacting frequencies are pretty low and are barely audible to us. To give you some idea of what 50 Hz is, my dog Buck gets this low growl (needs to be neutered) when other dogs walk by the house. His growl starts around 50 Hz.

Bass flies come in all varieties but the key is to create water disturbances with your lure and not your line. Quick, short retrieves with a surface-disturbing popper, like this freshwater bass fly, produce good results.

Dr. Arthur N. Popper (there's no shortage of irony in fish science), a scientist at University of Maryland, did the best lateral-line research anywhere. What he discovered in his laboratory was that a vibrational source (50-100 Hz) placed a few centimeters away from a trout's (bass and muskies too) lateral line will elicit an immediate change of direction and an attack by the fish. (I'd like to put a couple of those vibrational sources in my tackle box.)

I wonder if low frequency translates to slow lure retrieves? I've always wondered why a slow spinner retrieve seems to work

better than a fast one. And is there any reason to rattle plugs? What about a crustacean's clicking? These all have low-frequency components.

To incorporate some of Professor Popper's research into lure and fly construction consider this: In fly construction, a tube fly with a plastic body trailing other pieces of curvy plastic behind it might work great, if the wobble produced a low-vibratory sound on a sharp retrieve. The same goes for lures.

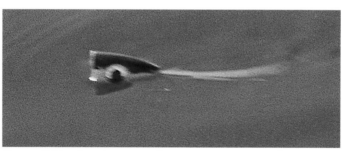

Popper fishing for saltwater predators.

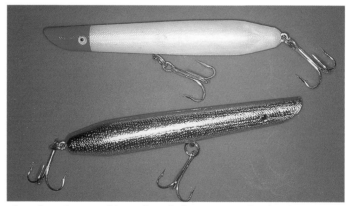

These "pencil poppers" have plastic balls incorporated within them, which attract fish by stimulating their lateral lines and inner ears. The front of the popper is scooped to create a wobbling action as it's retrieved. When experimenting with lateral-line stimulating materials, first start with low frequency vibrations by using slow retrieves. A slower retrieve won't be as likely to spook fish and you can always speed it up as you go.

Scary Stuff

"All our knowledge has its origin in our perceptions."

Leonardo da Vinci (1452-1519)

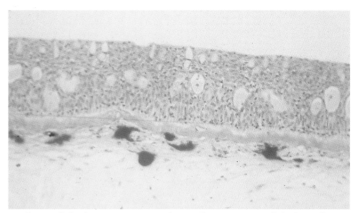

In this catfish skin-tissue section (viewed microscopically), the cells responsible for alarm cell substance release are the ones that look like the holes in Swiss cheese. The actual skin tissue is the reddish material. The alarm cell substances are contained in the "holes" or colorless areas. In salmonid species, it's thought that alarm cell substances are contained in specialized cells called club cells.

Ever wonder how bees get organized?

Me neither, until I discovered a hornet's nest while I was bushwhacking streamside one day. Actually, it started with a lone wasp or yellowjacket (order *Hymenoptera*) that wouldn't leave me alone so I summarily dispatched it with my hat.

Bad idea.

Apparently this was a scout on recon. And as he died, he transmitted my presence as a threat to the boys back at the hangar. Ten seconds post-mortem I was under siege by a squadron of angry hymenopterids stinging the daylights out of me.

But how did this lone sentry muster his cohorts for their airborne mission? Was it by insect ESP or through an ultra high-frequency beacon?

Actually, he did it by an evolutionary adaptation that enables release of compounds called alarm cell substances (see, baitfish aren't the only ones in on the alarm cell substance transmissions).

Alarm cell substances are substances released by both insects and fish as a way to communicate to the rest of the hive or school that trouble is a brewin'. How species respond to alarm cell substances depends on how they've come to rely on the mechanism.

Karl von Frisch first demonstrated fish alarm cell substances in 1941 when his experimental predator fish ate prey that released substances he termed "Schreckstoff" (a.k.a. "scary stuff", obviously Karl was a bait fisherman and prone to overstatement). Numerous studies since, have shown baitfish communicate with schoolmates by Schreckstoff, or alarm cell substances.

Baitfish won't gather up and attack like those bees did, but instead use chemical signals to signal a retreat. Pretty smart little fellers. A common alarm substance phenomenon that anglers will recognize is the "herring ball" response to predatory salmon.

SALMON SIGNAL

I've been fortunate to study with some of the best fish science researchers. One esteemed professor turned me on to this histological slide of catfish alarm cell substances. I asked him if salmonids had the same type of substances, he assured me they did. The notion of trout alarm cell substances, rings true to me. I think I've seen this in action when fly-fishing on the Beaverkill in upstate New York. The Beaverkill runs right through a town touting itself as Trout Town, USA. (T-town, a.k.a. Roscoe, New York, is where fly-fishing originated in the U.S.) While fishing one particular pool I observed about 15 brown trout lined up in accordance with Robert's Rule of Brown Trout Hierarchy.

I fished the tail of the pool with a Hendrickson (a nondescript brown fly) and began picking them off in series. After three sequentially upstream fish from the tail of the pool, I shot a cast to the head of the pool. I caught a nice 11-incher and proceeded to try the next fish that lie downstream.

Up until then, I had been doing great. It didn't matter how hard these downstream fish fought, once I caught a fish up front, you'd have thought my fly had halitosis. I couldn't get anything to budge, it was as if they had lockjaw. Were alarm cell substances involved? I suspect so. Alarm cell substances are a taste/smell method of communicating. When fishing running water, I anticipate fish downstream being put-off by their upstream brethren's alarm cell substances, ergo, this scenario, and others, has encouraged me to adhere to the "fish upstream" rule.

A practical application for angling with alarm cell substances. This live teaser fish releases alarm cell substances that attracts predators (which have evolved to recognize it).

My experience of lake fishing with surface flies also lends credence to my alarm cell substance hypothesis. As a result, I try to move around a little and not over-fish an area. I give the water a little time between targetings, and then come back a half-hour later, once the alarm cell substances dissipate.

Chapter Six

Behavior

"The nucleic acids invented human beings in order to be able to reproduce themselves even on the Moon."

Sol Spiegelman, quoted in Eigen 1992 p. 124

This hammerhead shark has anatomically dedicated so much of its evolution to sight that this Mexican fisher can literally pick it up by its optical tracts. Anatomical adaptations aren't always an advantage, as this hammerhead is finding out.

By looking in a craftsman's toolbox, you can usually tell what kind of work the tools perform. The same is true in nature. For example, animals that fly have wings.

An animal's hardware determines how it functions.

The social-science types get all worked up when scientists talk about this kind of thing. They say we're reductionists, appealing to modern man's attachment to having simple reasons to explain why we act the way we do. Still, without hardware, jobs can't get done.

Human beings have cortical brains. If I were to physically probe a particular area of your brain, you might suddenly smell Thanksgiving dinner. If I tickled a different drawer of your olfactory neurological "file cabinet," I would provoke yet another memory. Cortical brains allow for memory, reasoning and abstraction.

And here's the difference when it comes to brains: fish don't have cortexes.

This isn't bad news for fish. Absent this organ, life gets really simple. Ahhhhhh. . . Zen fish, live always in the present.

We attribute all sorts of cognition to them—like they're smart and crafty. In other words, we anthropomorphize.

Nature vs. nurture? Sometimes the environment a fish is in determines a fish's angling behavior and appearance. On the left are flies that are well-known steelhead flies and on the right, New Zealand trout flies. The flies are very similar but used to catch, often considered, different fish. Really, the only differences in the flies are the color hue and luminosity. The fly morphology is relatively similar.

Genetically closer to a brown trout, this Atlantic salmon looks a lot like its distant, Pacific salmon relatives. This is an example of the environment calling forth specific genetic characteristics.

We like doing that. Consider the lingering stories of lunker brown trout that are as wily as they are predatory—legends like these tell you more about those that love fish, than the creature themselves.

In fact, fish react very predictably and mechanically.

I suppose you could say that different races and species of fish have different "personalities," but in actuality particular traits are more likely a function of the fish's environment and its genetic makeup.

BIG BRAIN THEORY

How's this: One look at the brain of a fish and you can figure out how to catch it.

Sound ridiculous?

Well, actually I meant it to sound outrageous, but the concept helps illustrate a point. You really can tell what's important to a fish by looking at how much of the brain is dedicated to specific sensory functions.

Olfactory Lobes (smelling)

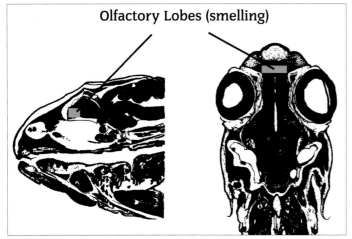

The olfactory lobes, within the telencephalon, are the part of the brain that manages the ability to smell.

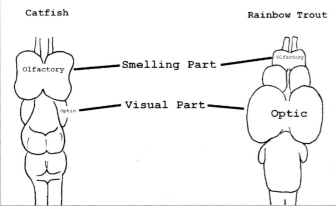

The size of the specific brain area, is proportional to the degree that the fish relies on its underlying function.

To begin with, a fish brain is about one-fifth the size of a similar-sized mammal's brain (this is the first clue that fish aren't brilliant). Small as it sounds, it's still subdivided into five parts.

The first part (going nose to tail) is the telencephalon; within

this lies an area called the olfactory lobe(s) which receives olfactory information (smells).

Sharks have huge telecephalons, along with correspondingly large olfactory lobes. So they can pick up scents at great distances. Catfish have big olfactory lobes when compared to trout; again the virtues of stinky bait.

To look at a salmonid brain, you'd notice the optic lobes predominating. This fits with common knowledge that trout, salmon and steelhead are big visual operators, along with a lot of other sportfish. If trout didn't have proportionally large optic lobes, I doubt that fly-fishing would be as developed as it is today, because flies are based primarily on visual cues. (Catfish and sharks have relatively poor eyesight compared to trout.)

THE REST OF THE BRAIN

Other than the sensory areas of the brain, the remainder is dedicated to those housekeeping processes (digestion, organ functioning, etc.) and motor functions (swimming). Pretty boring to anglers, rather exciting to fish physiologists.

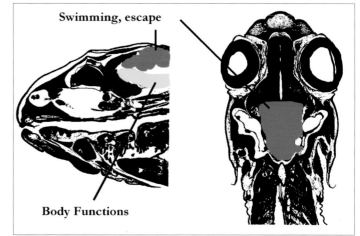

Fish life isn't all fun and play, there's always the day-to-day housekeeping responsibilities.

YOU ARE WHERE YOU LIVE?

Fish personality is best explained by primarily environment factors: physical and physiological, both of which can change.

I tried to entertain a largemouth bass that wouldn't give me the time of day, until I approached its nesting area, then it attacked anything I threw near it. For a similar reason, the tactics you employ for fishing salmon in salt water differ greatly from those you'll use during their freshwater migration.

Fishing for ocean-schooling species is still yet another phenomenon of environmental behavior. Knowing what's evolutionarily important to a species, given the environment they're in gives you insight into catching it (see sidebars this chapter).

VARIABLES

A Pacific salmon dies after its ocean migration as a consequence of major hormonal swings experienced during its pelagic journey. In a relatively short period of time, this salmon goes through hormonal surges from the thyroid, ovaries, testes and pituitary gland, just to name a few. We're talking major stress here.

Human beings aren't the only animals that have predictable behavior with hormonal swings. A salmon is much more likely to pick up a fly in the latter stages of its hormonal cycle. It does this out of a territorial response and more often than not, you'll catch a male defending its turf.

When the same fish was first sniffing fresh water in the estuary, you'd have a skittish character that was much harder to deceive. You don't have exaggerated territorial responses in the estuary, just pure nerves and reactions. Fishing for salmon in estuaries requires good presentations, clear lines, accurate casts and patience where farther up the salmon migratory road finesse is less critical.

To put it in humanistic terms: a fish's priorities change.

Estuarine fish are preparing to metabolically handle their freshwater future so they can make it up that river. Their river life is all about increasing the odds that their progeny will survive.

Survival of offspring is what motivates the spawning nest-sitting bass and the opportunistic bluegill trying to eat the baby bass. A bluegill cruising that pond is trying to tip the balance scale in its kids' favor, so they're the dominant species. Cruising roosterfish are insecure individuals, always staying close to their bluewater brethren, adhering to the safety-in-numbers rule.

Knowing what is important to a fish is the key to angling for it.

Know thy opponent.

Safety in numbers

"Defendit numerus: There is safety in numbers."

In J.R. Newman (ed.) The World of Mathematics, *New York: Simon and Schuster, 1956, p. 1452*

Have you ever wondered why people move to the country and then pack themselves in neighborhoods like the ones they came from? There's a biological precedence that explains this; it's safer.

And knowing this can catch you more fish. Groups of traveling fish are called schools (also known as shoals). A familiar example of this is herring, a favored baitfish of sportfish, including salmon.

From my point of view, watching herring is fascinating.

Mirrored sides flashing in the water with a periodic gleam of red gill; it's enough to mesmerize most observers. Interestingly enough, herring behavior has evolved to do just that, hypnotize predators. A herring alone becomes a target to predators, but a school of them produces a predatory headache, producing effects that confuse and even intimidate.

I can explain the confusion effect this way: Let's say it's Saturday, you're the predator, you're in the garage carrying a tackle bag filled with a lot of small stuff that rolls around, you know, beads, bobbers, drift things, weights, etc. Things are tense because your significant other is expected home soon and you should be doing something responsible like planning your SEP-IRA or mowing the lawn. As luck would have it, in rapid sequence, your gear bag breaks and your spouse hits the garage door opener. Panic grips you as you watch pieces of gear skittering across the floor like bugs fleeing from an overturned rock. For a split second, you (the predator) find yourself confused and hesitating before making the first retrieval effort. And therein lies the advantage to schooling; it produces a split-second delay in a predator's attack that makes the difference between survival and being eaten.

A camouflaged caribou herd in Alaska. So densely packed, they almost disappear into the far bank of the river. Caribou rely on safety in numbers.

Underlying the "nervous water", a pack of roosterfish are making chase in this series.

Stripping line furiously. . .

Nos sigue un pez! Fish on!

You can't believe how hard these fish fight. Now you're feeling better about the airfare, aren't you?

Methods of evasion vary among different species of bait-fish, but predator confusion has consistencies. Once tactic is the "bait ball" (see Chapter 6). The mirror effect created by reflective flashing makes it difficult for a predator to pick out a specific individual, thereby protecting the school as a whole.

Fish working in numbers (schooling, balling up) is another example of a hardware-determined behavior. Each baitfish uses their lateral lines to feel where his classmates are located. It's also theorized that some fish use their visual ability to pick up reflected polarized light from their neighbors (see Chapter 4). This light-perception hardware allows them to position themselves in close proximity to their wingman, or fin-man as the case may be.

Schooling fish will often act as predators and avoid predators at the same time. An angler fishing for roosterfish in Baja can use an understanding of this to advantage. Roosterfish travel together. Quite often you'll see a cruising pack of "nervous water" before you get a take (see photos).

Putting a fly in front of an excited rooster gets all its buddies worked up too. This sets up a competitive feeding situation (see sidebar 2) and more often than not, you'll hook one. But the schools move pretty quickly and by the time you boat that fish, his cohorts are gone. Then you have to pick up and search for the next pack.

Here's where knowledge of schooling fish behavior makes you more productive.

KEEP YOUR FIRST FISH IN THE WATER

I guess to a rooster fish, "out of sight, out of mind," but as long as a fish stays on the line and in the water, the pack won't leave the area. Don't worry too much about stressing your prisoner: Like other saltwater species, these guys are really tough, so it won't harm them to play them for a brief period.

Mob Mentality

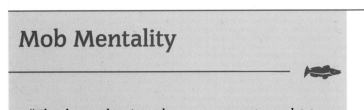

"The hypothesis: what we accept ought to explain phenomena, which we have observed. But they ought to do more than this: our hypotheses ought to foretell phenomena, which have not yet been observed."

William Whewell (1794-1866)
English mathematician, philosopher.

ENVY

Where did this whole computer and Internet technology come from? First I hear that sooner or later every home in North America is going to have its own personal computer, then, before I know it, I'm falling behind schedule because I'm not familiar with the "Windows platform."

Okay, so during my continuing education a cadre of graduate school types pounded the Windows thing into my middle-aged psyche. Why do I still feel like I'm looking at the future through the keyhole?

Seems there's a technology feeding-frenzy and I wasn't invited to the party. Even my buddy Dean, the car mechanic extraordinaire turned stockbroker, is in on the kill.

I've heard of new money, but nanosecond money? What's up with that? It makes me angry! I want some too. There's a bait-ball out there getting hammered and I'm not even in the water.

RATIONALIZING ENVY

I saw the irony in that perspective while preparing notes on fish behavior. I'm like the fish that perceives a scarcity of resources in its environment. Even when there's enough food around, bring a few more mouths into the picture and you've got a competitive situation, whether we're talking human beings or cold-blooded creatures. Competitive feeding is a very real phenomenon, which often goes unnoticed because of the occult nature of underwater life. We don't often see the fish before we catch it, and if we do see the take, we usually can't tell what's happening in the fish community from which it came.

If we could observe the dynamics that transpire within a fish's population, the reason why a fish did or didn't take the offering would become more predictable and practical to anglers.

COMPETITION IS GOOD FOR THE MARKET

Lars and Buck go through this competitive feeding thing. Lars (the slightly pudgy 8-year-old Norwegian elkhound) bullies his buddy, Buck, the affable Lab, every morning at breakfast. Lars may not even be hungry, but he just can't bring himself to let Buck eat breakfast in peace. As soon as Jan places the two bowls of kibble on the floor, Lars keeps an evil eye on Buck and proceeds to pilfer from the Labrador's bowl. Buck avoids eye contact, wouldn't think of going to Lars' bowl, and whines like a big baby. Then he starts barking in protest.

Trout do this, just with less whining and barking.

COMPETITIVE FEEDING

Cold water slows everything down—from steelhead fishing to intracellular enzymatic processes. When the temperature falls, fish move in slow motion. It doesn't matter whether you're fishing for bass, panfish, trout or steelhead; coldwater angling requires some careful strategizing.

Remember the Optimal Foraging Theory (OFT), which in simplified terms warns: don't do it if it's not worth it. We have this behavior ingrained. In "fish reality" this translates to "whatever prey you chase better be worth more energy than you have to expend getting it." In cold water, fish have to expend a lot more energy to move, not to mention the basic cost of chasing elusive prey. This means: in cold water, presenting an imitation directly to the fish increases your chance of deception.

There is a way to improve your odds when coldwater fishing, or in any water temperature for that matter. Use competitive feeding to your advantage. This is a lot like the auction theory of angling (my theory): The more bidders you get, the more likely you are to get someone to bite. Angling experience bears out this prediction.

One February, I was fishing in 36-degree water for steelhead. It was darn cold and the fly-fishing was dead. I could bump a fish's head with all the known successful fly patterns with no takers. I switched to a big-bladed, slow-moving spinner, and still no results. . .that is, until I created a competitive feeding situation.

When I started fishing an area that had more than one fish holding. I wouldn't place the lure as near as I would a fly, but pretty close anyway. I had much more success triggering the dominant fish's strike response when there was a subordinate fish behind.

It reminded me of Lars: exerting his dominance over Buck in a survival-based behavior.

Competition served this steelhead well, until this scientific angler took advantage of his piscine personality. This soon-to-be-released steelhead was coaxed to the lure because it had to outperform its buddies.

Crypto Trout

Sasquatch, Skunk Apes and Yeti are charter members. Nessie, the Loch Ness monster, was the first one. There's no shortage of legends—urban, aquatic or otherwise. We're curious about strange creatures and their habits. Scholars called Cryptozoologists spend their professional lives searching for and documenting heretofore unverified animals.

Anglers are Cryptozoologists of a sort. Incessantly looking for the big fish of myth. With names like "Old Pete" or "Uncle Charlie," these unverified piscine celebrities stubbornly remain hidden, and go by lots of names, but always the-big-one-that-got-away.

So I ask the question, "How do these big fish become so big?" Certainly not by acting like other fish. No, they do it their way. And they have something in common beyond size and craft: they dine on creatures with backbones. They're meat eaters and they're hidden.

Are there 36-inch brown trout cruising your neighborhood? Fisheries scientists electro-shock sections of streams, wacko anglers don wetsuits and flippers looking for narcoleptic leviathans, but do they ever see all the fish? Do they document the really big ones?

Doubtful.

Anglers catch small fish mostly. You could look at this a couple of ways. Either there aren't many big ones around to catch, or they get smart and are hard to tempt. It's easier to say there aren't big ones anymore justifying our angling results, our egos being as sensitive as they are. But both are true.

"Okay, if Crypto Trout (CTs) do exist, how would I find one and go about catching one?" you say.

Getting to them may just be a simple matter of caloric arithmetic. The optimal foraging theory predicts that a fish will always try to be on the winning side of the dietary benefit-for-expenditure seesaw. "Get the most nutrition for your buck," is the credo.

How would they do that? Well, an exclusive diet of invertebrates is out. Even Murray, the local hardware store manager, knows that "only the little guys go for dry flies."

"Wait a minute," you say, "I've caught some nice-sized fish on dry flies."

Ah, but maybe they were small compared to the Cryptos in that water.

Fact is, you've got to have baitfish, big baitfish—something with ribs that will stick to yours, to build the kind of terminators I'm talking about.

(Some Crypto Trout don't limit their diet to fish; a few partake of other species like mammals and birds.)

The scientific method allows for the Crypto Trout theory. The world-record stripers (largemouth bass also) are caught on life-sized rubber rainbow trout imitations. Most species of big game fish are caught on baitfish imitations. CTs can be caught in a similar manner, but to tie one on you'll need to match it up with a worthy opponent and send an offer it can't refuse.

THE PLAN

To catch the hidden one, start big. Research supports the big bait/big fish theory. Tie on a big pattern. Set the alarm early (herein lies the reason I haven't caught these guys), the invertebrate drift is higher in the morning crepuscular hours than the evening. This means the little trout are out feeding on insects and the Sasquatch salmonids are dining on them.

Incorporate a few good vibrations into your lure. Use something that makes a ruckus and colors that stimulate the strike response (see Chapter 9).

I know it's dark out and you can't see what you're doing, but

This 20-inch lake cutthroat got so big by cannibalizing its 8-inch cutthroat relatives. Getting big is serious business, especially for little fish.

Ever eaten so much you got sick? This trout did. The rainbow on the bottom appears darker because of melanosis, a skin pigment reaction to stress in fish.

This rainbow was 16-17 inches. Crypto Trout don't eat only vertebrates like themselves, a few other species (mammals, birds, etc.) add variety to their diets.

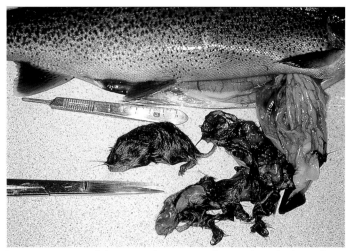

On examination of the stomach contents, three rodents (red eared voles, I suspect) were discovered. Makes sense for anglers to fish with those vertebrate patterns now, doesn't it?

that's good, because it also means Big Bob the brown trout, can't see you either. But be careful! Bob sees better in low light than other trout species. You might want to do a little pre-maneuver reconnaissance to get the lay of the land so he doesn't notice you.

They're flying blind in the aqueous clouds and relying on instruments for a successful mission. Cast deftly, retrieve noisily and slowly. These ninjas of the night use their sense of smell and lateral lines to navigate and feed.

I know these techniques work because I've conversed with successful Crypto Trout hunters. I met one, who shall remain anonymous, in Island Park, Idaho about 10 years ago. Heard of specialists in California, but they're not talking—something about the code of the Crypto Hunters (a.k.a. Eastern Sierra "Brown Baggers").

Yeah, yeah. . . You're warriors and you have to stay invisible like the quarry you pursue.

That's fine, but some of us are idealists, new to the discipline, and we want to join the ranks of the converted. We're informed, we're committed and we're armed with big baitfish lures and flies, so if that's one of you silent vets I've just bumped into this dark morning. . . move over.

Tying patterns for Cryptos.

Chapter Seven

Heresy

"In Science the credit goes to the man who convinces the world, not to the man to whom the idea first occurred."

Sir William Osler (1849-1919), Canadian physician

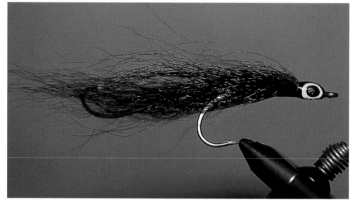

Good examples of target enhancement or contrast, black flies and lures produce good contrast in various backgrounds.

Definition: Her-e-sy/n. (pl. –sies) 1 belief or practice contrary to orthodox doctrine. 2 nonconforming opinion.

Well, that quote covers this chapter pretty succinctly.

When I first started fly-fishing years ago, I was told that the "best" way to fly-fish was to cast dry flies. It wasn't for a year or two that I heard about nymphing. But strict adherence to dry-fly angling didn't make sense in light of what stomach-pump results revealed about the average fish. Mostly their diet comprised subsurface prey.

Dry flies, nymphs, matching hatches. . . is this the totality of prey imitation? Consider for a moment, that it's quite possible a lot of anglers don't really know what's important to the prey they pursue. We often think that fish, especially trout, care about a hatch being matched. So we go out, observe what they're eating, try to match it, catch a few fish and leave, flush with egocentric smugness.

I'm proposing that even though matching the hatch does make a difference, there might be more to it than meets the eye.

ANGLING PROPHESY

Lee Wulff rocked the dogma boat a while back. Initially, I didn't know what to make about his conclusions. Lee was quite the sportsman and a pretty articulate guy. He fished a lot in Upstate New York, where American fly-fishing was practiced on classic rivers like the Willowemoc and Beaverkill.

I was told that he didn't believe trout could see colors, but when I read his book *Trout on a Fly*, I discovered that wasn't what he said at all.

To quote Lee, *"The chance that trout see color exactly as we do is, I believe, extremely slim. And what does that do to all the color-concentrating fly fishermen and fly tyers? It should shake them a little. If we found out that trout could not see color at all that would really drive us bonkers."*

Wulff goes on to state *"A trout's ability to see and recognize colors as we see them is one thing; but to know what he (the trout) can see is another and a more important matter."*

You get the point: it's not what we see, but what the trout sees and considers important that interests us.

Although he was wrong about the color thing, Lee had visionary insight in approaching angling from the fish's context. Trout do see colors quite well, however their interpretation of what color means is most likely different from ours.

Lee goes on to say that he considered the most important issue to be contrast. He alluded to this by saying, *"concentrate on the light and dark aspects for effectiveness."* When you think of the state of fish retinal research, at the time he wrote his book (1986), his conclusions on contrast were prophetic.

MATCH THE HARDWARE

Instead of matching the insect hatch via color, size, shape and behavior, I suspect we'll be closer to what matters to a trout if we look at their physiological hardware. Fish come with brains, retinas and optic lobes, let's match what their equipment is designed to see.

One sensory organ that transmits a lot of information to the neurological command center is the eye, and when you look at fish eye structure, it appears that what matter's most to trout, is determining whether an object is predator/prey or not.

How do they do that?

IN GENERAL: HOW FISH DETERMINE PREY

Predator/prey discrimination, also known as target detection, is the basic fish survival question.

Example: A fish sees something and asks **target-detection question #1**: *"Is what I'm looking at a predator/prey target?"*

From a target-detection context, a rock wouldn't be considered a target to a fish, but a baitfish or predator would. Question #1 is answered yes or no. If no, keep swimming, if **yes**. . . Go on to the next fish survival question:

Example: Fish asks **target acceptability question #2**: *"Given that this observed object is a predator/prey target, is it one worth eating?"*

The second question is a qualifier of the first: is this an acceptable target? If the answer to #2 lies within this fish's eating parameters (prey), it will go for it, because fish are in the eating business. If it's within the parameter for a predator, the fish will avoid. . . but we're focusing on matching prey items here.

Things like food scarcity, potential nutritional value and competition can add pressure to the question of acceptability. What isn't acceptable to one animal is to another under a different set of circumstances.

Let's take a closer look "inside" of each of these questions and see what it means to a designing scientific angler.

CLOSER LOOK: TARGET DETECTION (QUESTION #1) = MORPHOLOGY + LUMINOSITY

We want to design an imitation that will first be considered a prey target (to answer target-detection question #1, **yes**) by the species we're interested in. The most important criterion in target detection for a visual predator, such as the trout we're seeking, is **outline**. The primary characteristic of a target outline is shape or size (i.e. 3-dimensional silhouette), otherwise known as **morphology**. To anglers, this is the most important criterion imitation.

It's common sense really, because if we don't get morphology into the acceptable range, we don't (usually) progress.

COMPLETING QUESTION #1: TARGET DETECTION. . . LUMINOSITY OVER COLOR

Once we've passed the 3-D morphology part of the question, a major component of prey appearance is luminosity: the quality of reflected light. This relates to the light/dark attributes of the overall target morphology that Lee alluded to (also see Chapter 7 sidebar 2, countershading). Of course there will be different luminous qualities for different species of prey, but what a fish ultimately sees is prey-reflected light producing an outline and, within it, gradients of luminosity.

WHAT ABOUT COLOR?

Taken separately, color is less important than luminosity, although it contributes to it.

How do I know this?

Because the cone mosaics in trout retinas function first to create target enhancement. This makes sense when you think about where fish live: under water. It gets dark down there, especially at the crepuscular hours (dawn and dusk) and light, sometimes in only minute amounts, is at a premium. Distinguishing fine gradients of light is important. What's also of interest is that the dawn and dusk hours have the least light yet the most feeding going on. These periods coincide with the maximal invertebrate drift, which is the twice daily, high concentrations of drifting invertebrates. Evolution taught insects to survive by migrating in low light periods, yet she rewarded fish that successfully identified the crepuscular travelers!

Remember, when light is restricted (e.g. dawn and dusk), colors don't show up well. If survival depended on keen color discrimination at dawn, all the world's trout would be dead by evolutionary high noon. To me, the research suggests that trout (and probably lots of other fish) use luminosity, more than color, to detect prey and predators as targets.

I'm not saying color doesn't play a substantial role, it does. Quite often, especially during times of prey selectivity (picky trout), it can make all the difference whether a fish takes your fly or not.

Which reminds me of a story.

I remember noticing from the corner of my eye, a rise on a roadside pond while driving through Yellowstone Park in 1989. Without hesitation, I pulled over and grabbed my 6-weight, which was pre-loaded with a floating line and a size-16 Elk Hair Caddis.

I approached the pond-edge while false casting my fly towards the rise. The water was so clear that I could see the fish 10 feet below, turn and look at my fly. Responding to my presentation, it shot to within three feet of my fly and just hung there, inspecting. Just as suddenly, it turned heel without a strike. I cast a couple more times and on the third try, the fish took my fly.

What does this tell me? The fish was interested in my fly from the outset but I had some convincing to do. Like adolescents, fish don't have a lot of behavior that is related to anything other than feeding and reproduction, so I'm assuming it suspected my fly was prey but there took some convincing in the final inspection... like, this might be prey, but is it the "right prey"?

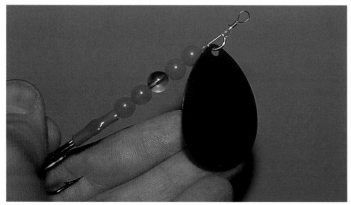

A little black spray paint transformed this spinner into a good contrasting blade.

When this spoon (previously seen) is viewed on a brown background (like off-color water), the black shows up better than the brass reflective tape.

How fish determine "the right prey" is the second major fly-creation criteria.

TARGET ACCEPTABILITY (QUESTION #2) = COLOR + BEHAVIOR

For any type of criteria a fish might use to judge prey or predators (or even mates for that matter), there's going to be a range that's acceptable, and outside that range the imitation will be rejected. Acceptability criteria would be those characteristics that say, "Not only am I realistic on first impression, but other things increase my acceptability."

Fly color and behavior (but not luminosity or intensity) would be included in target-acceptability parameters. Color, hue and behavior can help seal the deal but if the target is out of range, morphology or luminosity wise, these acceptability criterions won't help.

What's with separating out target detection and target acceptability, you ask?

WHICH IS MORE IMPORTANT: TARGET DETECTION OR ACCEPTABILITY?

Target detection is the most important. Knowing the difference between target detection and acceptability, you can often bypass the secondary target acceptability hurdle by overloading the target-detection criteria, therefore triggering a strike reaction.

For example, lures do this. So do attractors to a lesser degree. A lot of lures don't look anything like prey, but they might generate enough concern about their being a predator that they threaten fish into striking out of reflex.

A good example of target-detection overload is a fluorescent chartreuse spinner. What's this matching? Spinner blades vibrate and make low-frequency sounds and flash like guanine scales with the net result being a lot of attention-getting commotion. How long would you want to hang around and determine if this flashing vibrating thing coming at you is for real or not? Not long, I'd guess.

Attractor flies will trigger strike responses. Some flies work well but don't match anything in particular, yet they get through the first door (target detection) and trigger the trout's strike response. Color is often used as an attractor, the most common color being red.

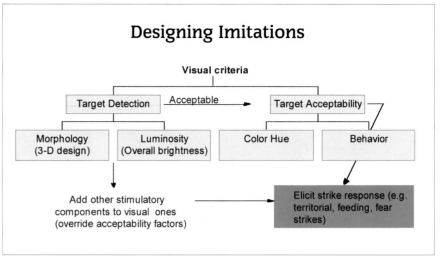

Designing Imitations

A salmonid's visual equipment is physiologically designed to quickly provide target information. As anglers, we want to design lures and flies (targets) that fish will strike.

Given this, I would think that a fly like a Royal Wulff would work pretty well.

A Royal Wulff has an iridescent peacock herl (which reflects polarized light like crazy), and when viewed under water from more than a yard, appears to have a gray spot in the center. Suddenly, as the fly approaches, the gray center turns out to be bright red floss! The last time you (remember, you're a trout here) saw a bright-red abdomen like this was during stickleback breeding season, when those three-spined males really bugged you by flashing their "I'm in the mood for love" red coloration.

You'll strike.

ATTRACTOR REVIEW

With a successful attractor pattern that includes a little red, you have correct 3-dimensional morphology within overall prey (insect) parameter range and now it's blinking red at you (like an obnoxious baitfish). It's a great combination.

SUM IT UP

To create an imitation, I use the following guide:

1) **Target Detection**: Morphology and luminosity.
   - **Morphology** = Size, 3-D shape
   - **Luminosity** = Shading. Shading translates to areas with differential gradients of reflection (think of this first in black and white or shades of gray).

2) **Target acceptability**: Color hue and behavior.
   - Color hue is self explanatory, holding the luminosity of the color materials constant (intensity relates to luminosity). Bright pink is more luminous than dull pink, though the color hue can be the same.
   - Behavior is a big criterion here. For dry-fly selective fish, minimizing drag is a must. The real thing doesn't drag. If you're skating a bomber, then skating becomes attraction via triggering, but it's still behavior. A chronomid just barely floats up the water column, behavior here is important: a slow retrieve is in order. In the shallows, a fast retrieve on a baitfish or leech pattern for the crepuscular brown predator is consistent with the real thing in nature. Slow is counterproductive here.

Patterned after a Yellow Butt Skunk, this attractor pattern uses small amounts of red, has contrasting colors, fluorescence and reflective properties.

Painful Reminder

"Study nature, love nature, stay close to nature. It will never fail you."

Frank Lloyd Wright, architect

Members of the order Hymenoptera, bees and wasps also incorporate color superstimuli and contrast.

In summers past, my chocolate lab Mulligan used to go crazy trying to bite the yellowjackets hovering around his food bowl. He kept this up until one day he got a mouthful o' wasp and learned a big lesson.

Don't bite yellowjackets.

His subsequent fat lip was a reminder that he wasn't physiologically equipped to take advantage of fine *Hymenoptera* dining, like fish can.

Wasps and bees are members of the class *Hymenoptera*, and they can really pack a wallop in their sting. The sting is created by a painful injection of polypeptide toxins or proteins and other low molecular weight compounds delivered by the insect's "stinger."

Most of us know bees sting, but apparently fish don't care. But why not? Why does it seem that fish can do with impunity what you or I, and other mammals (like Mulligan), cannot?

Is there a possible angling advantage embedded in this mystery?

A bee or wasp will often sting if you disturb their home. Bees and wasps (including yellowjackets) build nests under eaves, in shrubs, and other prime *Hymenoptera* habitats: like rotten tree stumps. Once the nest is molested, the first insects rousted release alarm substances much like fish do (see Chapter 5). This works to incite the rest of the nest into a riot. Now you've got a bunch of cranky bees, or wasps, all worked up and looking for someone to take it out on.

The *Hymenoptera* use their stinging ability to defend themselves and kill prey. Their venom is injected through the skin (integument) via the venomous gland-connected stinger. Once anointed, we get stung and it hurts unless we've developed immunity to the toxin (like many beekeepers). Not so with fish. A fish has a couple of formidable barriers even though its skin is quite tender and sensitive compared to terrestrial mammals.

WHAT LIES BETWEEN FISH AND BEES

The aquatic environment provides protection from airborne insects. So fish don't worry about wasp stings to their skin (scales, mucus, etc). But a fish can partake of a wasp, bee or ant with relish. An insect sting doesn't damage their mouth (called the pharynx) because it has a built-in bony barrier, covered by tough skin. The pharynx functions as a crushing tool and even some fish pulverize shell-covered prey for a living.

"Okay, Mr. Smart Guy," you mutter, "that handles the mouth or pharynx, but I've been the recipient of a car-window-impacted wasp's last stinging hurrah on the highway of life.

A little exaggeration in this imitation.

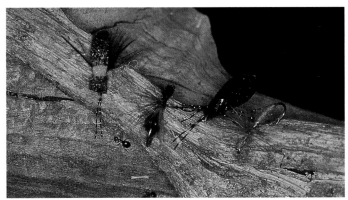

Ants are also a member of Hymenoptera, There's a couple of the genuine articles just below the branch holding the imitations. Fish like these guys too.

Why wouldn't a fish's delicate esophagus and digestive tract be just as sensitive to this possibility?"

GOOD QUESTION

To understand this, it's best to briefly outline the sting reaction in mammals.

When a bee stings us, it injects its venom beneath our epidermal (skin) covering. The toxic venom causes a mammal's tissue-based white blood cells (called basophils) to release histamine and other inflammatory compounds. That's why if you get stung, your doctor may recommend you take antihistamines like Benadryl to counteract the inflammatory reaction.

Well, one difference between fish and mammals is that fish don't have tissue basophils and as a result there isn't a release of inflammatory histamine (contained in basophils). No release of inflammatory compounds, no inflammation.

ANGLING PERSPECTIVE

From an evolutionary point of view, it would be pretty keen to be able to take advantage of a prey source that no one else could. I think anglers have come to appreciate the benefit that ants (stings derived from formic acid) provide the fly-fisher who chooses to hurl terrestrial imitations. So why not more bee imitations?

Anglers for the most part don't utilize the stinging members of *Hymenoptera* as much as they could. I think that this might be due again to our seeing the world through our eyes, instead of through the piscine paradigm.

To us, bees and wasps are noxious creatures. To fish, they're prey.

Using a Brain to Design Flies

"Like the song says 'teach your children' to go fishing with their minds."

Jimmy Buffet: Beach House on the Moon

The way a forensic scientist goes about recreating past events is by examining the evidence and piecing them all together with a plausible scenario (see Hills criteria, Chapter 9). For example, imagine that we're at an archeological dig some time in the future. We're investigating the remains of an ancient tribe of anglers that fished in the early 2000s. We know they're anglers because of the petrified angling tools embedded in the exposed excavation. Shimano, Abel, Hardy, Orvis, Powerbait. . . You can tell a lot about a civilization by the tools it has.

So what tools do fish have?

The primary tool a fish uses in the business of survival is its brain. A fish's gray matter receives its information in the form of neurological impulses from a complex array of sensors. A fish's eyes convert retinal binary on/off patterns from reflected images of pigment activation into data that is interpreted by the optic lobes of the brain. Smells and tastes are no more than olfactory/gustatory parcels of scents that trigger chemical-sensing receptors, which informs the olfactory lobe that there's a tasty visitor in the area. These are the tools fish use.

These exquisitely sensitive sensory organs are connected to a fish's brain which functions a lot like a microprocessor. The brain coordinates the agenda: Fight or Flight, attack or pass on confrontation. More like evolutionary derived reactions than decisions, a fish responds, only to the degree it can assimilate the sensory information with its brain.

Why then, are we fly tiers sensory snobs?

We create flies with limited visual criteria. It's outdated, incomplete and incomprehensible if you begin to look at the structure of the organ that dictates how a fish will respond. An educated angler and fly tier could match their creation to a fish's ability to sense. The way to discern a fish's ability to sense our imitation is to examine its brain.

When you look at a rainbow trout's brain, what you notice is its big optic lobes (see diagram below). Trout are primarily visual feeders and their brains corroborate that predilection. In tying flies for trout or any salmonid, attention to visual criteria, like 3-D morphology, is important. If fly-fishers want to start catching species with poorer eyesight, upon examining their brains we'll find out that they make up for a lack of visual acuity with enhancement of other senses.

Mentioned earlier, a catfish could use a guide dog to get around under water. Cats can't see worth beans, but they can taste their way out of just about any situation. These barbeled torpedoes have taste buds all over their body and subsequently they literally rub up on their objects of interest. For some reason a lot of fly-fishers turn up their noses at using gustatory and olfactory (taste and smell) stimulants. But wait! I think there's opportunity here. We could try to make imitation scents and tastes that combine gustatory triggers. We've heard it helps sell

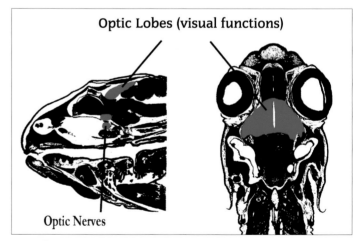

Optic Lobes (visual functions)

Optic Nerves

Lots of tissue dedicated to the visual issue.

a house if the smell of recently baked bread or cookies greets prospective buyers. Do we think we're all that different from fish? Let's sell some flies!

Traditional fly tiers are incorporating vibratory components in their flies already. It's not always acknowledged but setting up those "good vibrations" has been going on for quite a while. Let's get serious and create some shapes and structures that really get those ossicles and lateral lines singing! We can incorporate slit tubes, flippers and flutterers just like nature has. Instead of using nature's collagen, fibrin, cartilage and epidermis, we'll use plastics, feathers, fur and metals in sensory-stimulating ways!

Chapter Eight

The Predator/Prey Relationship

"The producers would like to thank all the fish who have taken part in this film. We hope that other fish will follow the example of those who have participated, so that, in the future, fish all over the world will live together in harmony and understanding and put aside their petty differences, cease pursuing and eating each other, and live for a brighter better future for all fish and those who love them."

Monty Python, The Meaning of Life

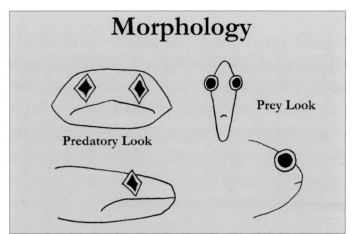

Big round eyes and a small mouth are good prey characteristics. Predatory features like broad head, big mouths, large, ringed elliptical eyes intimidate and frighten fish. Creeps me out a little too.

PREDATORS

Are you frightening fish with your lures and imitations?

I know I've scared a few and I bet you have too. I didn't know why until I learned something about the morphology and the relationship between of predators and prey.

Predators have certain things in common. Some search for prey, some wait for prey to come to them, but most have a common predatory appearance. You know...they look mean.

We humans interpret meanness or aggression in certain ways. For example, when people frown, their mouths are downturned and we have an instinctive reaction to this. The opposite is also true. If someone smiles, it puts us more at ease. Apparently, in some ways we aren't much different than fish (this is good news). Fish have learned to take faces seriously too.

Facial features are important across the animal kingdom. Eye shape is a prime feature of all vertebrate (animals with backbones) faces. Nice big round eyes make us comfortable, large angular, slanted and narrowly focused eyes intimidate us. It's the same with fish. Scientists have found that certain predatory features like broad heads, wide downturned mouths and ringed elliptical eyes elicit fright responses in prey fishes. Take a look at the illustration and see for yourself.

You can use eye morphology to increase the chances of a strike response: take a look at Chapter 9, sidebar 1.

RISKY BUSINESS

Nature punishes unreasonable risk-takers. The risk/opportunity ratio seems to be calculated very carefully for fish. If something looks like a big dietary score, that's great, go for it. But if going for the big kill is going to put you at undue risk, then you just may want to pass on the opportunity. The only time a predatory fish will edge out on a limb is when it comes time to mate. Then they will leap from leaf to leaf, so to speak. See, people really aren't that much different than fish.

It's usually counterproductive to make an imitation look menacing, so you want to avoid creating a predatory impression, and make them appear more prey-like.

BAITFISH PREY

In general, we're trying to imitate prey, but what determines the overall appearance?

Knowing your targeted species and their baitfish of preference is key to creating convincing imitations. Some baitfish are so translucent all you might notice are eyes, brain and gonads. The remainder of the body is clear.

Many ocean-dwelling baitfish are silver-sided and laterally flattened or compressed. This renders the species close to invisible in water: in effect, they act as mirrors, imaging the surrounding environment in a fashion that makes them seem to disappear.

Most baitfish incorporate both countershading and reflective properties. Part of the reason for countershading is while most aquatic light tends to be downwelling (i.e. flowing down from the sky in a vertical plane), the primary illumination of a baitfish from a predator's perspective, comes from the side. This light, called horizontal spacelight, is only about 5% as intense, overall, as the downwelling rays, but significantly more important. (For more details of how countershading works, see sidebar 2.) Countershading is nature's camouflaging response to differences in illumination.

Salmon alevins (sacfry), with translucent bodies, round black eyes and a contrasting orange yolk sac. Flies imitating these produce well.

Because reflective and countershaded prey become invisible, predators have had to come up with something that allows them to distinguish the mirror on the wall, or the baitfish in the water.

LUMINOSITY AGAIN:

Arnold Schwarzenegger appeared in a movie called "Predator," in which he was pitted against an alien that camouflaged itself by visually mirroring the Central American jungle through which it traveled, thereby becoming nearly invisible. The operative word here is "nearly." What you, as a viewer, could see was an alien-shaped outline that slightly distorted light.

Fish watch the same movie, more or less. It's a jungle down there, and they have to hunt the invisible, only for them it's prey that's hard to see.

Baitfish reflect their watery surroundings with reflective guanine and hypoxanthine crystalline scales. How do predators differentiate the countershaded, mirror-sided baitfish from the surroundings? The chrome-like reflection comes from the cellular incorporation of guanine and hypoxanthine crystalline materials into scales. How do predators differentiate the countershaded, mirror-sided baitfish from the surroundings?

It's all a matter of contrast.

CONTRAST AND COMPARE

If you're a baitfish hoping to blend into the background, you don't want a lot of contrasting colors, you want mirrored sides. As mentioned earlier, reflection allows you to blend into the surroundings like Arnold's alien. Hunters of baitfish need to overcome their preys' illusion of invisibility and many have.

Predatory fish view their environment, including their prey, in gradients or progressive shades of reflection or luminosity. The guanine scales of baitfish reflect light, such as polarized light, which is associated with prey (see Chapter 4 sidebar 2). What this presents is a differential luminosity, kind of like a fish outline or bright spot in the mirror. It is this "contrast in luminosity" or photocontrast, that allows a predator to see its prey.

The predator's ability to distinguish prey luminosity is a significant concept to the scientific angler. The trick is to work it to our advantage—to see from their perspective.

To accomplish this, the specific baitfish you're imitating

and the nature of the aquatic environment you're fishing in will dictate the quality and degree of luminosity you choose to use. In open-ocean and estuary fishing, incorporate brighter reflections and use colors in the smaller wavelengths including UV-reflective materials.

As you move into fresh water and more turbid conditions, baitfish luminosity decreases in the naturals and takes on more of the coloration of breeding fish. Where bright silvery scales persisted in marine conditions, you'll now see more brassy or tarnished looking reflections (like perch imitations) which are consistent with the color shift to the longer wavelengths that occurs within the water itself.

EXCEPTION TO THE LUMINOSITY

There is what appears to be an exception to the luminosity rule which actually proves it. It also explains a common phenomenon that most anglers have experienced.

Largemouth bass are efficient predators. . . they don't fool around. Hunting visually and utilizing lateral lines, bass attack first and ask questions later. Now consider the context in which they operate. In small ponds and lakes there are typically schools of bass-prey, like bluegill, perch and sticklebacks. These schools of baitfish often create a type of "confusion effect" I wrote about earlier, similar to the bewilderment you may have experienced when using a small dipnet to catch a particular minnow among many dashing about in a bait well. When they all look alike, chasing a particular one becomes pretty difficult.

If an individual in a school, however, looks strikingly different from the others, it creates what's called the "stranger effect." For example, if two of the hundred or so baitfish were blue, instead of silvery, the blue guys would stand out in the crowd. The stranger effect (predicted by the well-known stranger theory) predicts that the blue individuals are more likely to get eaten by the bass than any silver individual. And that's exactly what happens.

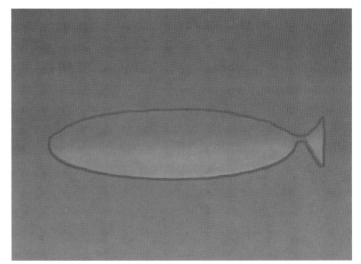

Countershading is a way fish hide. The fish scales reflect light in the same degree that light shines on the fish, making the fish appear to disappear. The outline on this countershaded illustration is to aid readers. . . fish retinas have their own way of determining outlines of near-invisible prey (target enhancement).

We could actually guess this would happen from what we know about fish retinas. The blue baits show up differently in the bass's visual context. They contrast with the silvery mass, allowing preferential focus—thereby eliminating some of the confusion (effect) created by the school. In this case the photo contrast or difference in luminosity isn't one of a background of dimmed luminosity, with a bright prey-spot of luminance, but a dark spot (blue individual) on a background of brightness (other baitfish in the school).

That's why a scientific angler will always include a few strangers in their gearbox.

LUMINOSITY AND INVERTEBRATE PREY

All sorts of game fish feed on invertebrates. Scuds and bugs, shrimp to water fleas, these creatures are the mainstays of many predatory fish diets from bluegill to bass, sockeye to chinook, or some other salmonid.

Surprise: Many of these spineless creatures reflect light. Start a collection, get out your polarized filtered flashlight and take a look. Or instead, examine images of brine shrimp taken through the polarizing lens of a microscope: nearly translucent to the naked human eye, here they suddenly shine bright as stars.

Salmonids Change Their Point of View

"According to convention there is a sweet and a bitter, a hot and a cold, and according to convention there is order. In truth there are atoms and a void."

Democritus (400 B.C.)

A migrating salmon's list of potential predators and prey is formidable. In a salmon's birthgrounds, the fry must fear being eaten by trout (herons, kingfishers, otters, et al), not to mention squawfish, other salmon species, steelhead, those pesky small-mouth bass and irritating panfish seen in warmer water downstream.

As the salmon smolt starts its ocean migration, it must develop new skills while encountering dangers, like marine mammals and simultaneously learn to eat off a changing menu, including herring, anchovies and squid.

On the return trip, the prodigal fish deals with an entirely different set of freshwater dilemmas, like bears and eagles. A migrating salmon has to deal with a tremendous amount of strife compared to the non-anadromous fish, say one just hanging out in a lake.

How is this an advantage?

Well, I guess it all depends on where you're coming from.

I don't mean you as an angler or reader; I mean you as the returning salmon. Oceans are great for fish. Scientists propose that salmon originated in fresh water and became accustomed to the marine environment so they could take advantage of the huge resources the ocean held.

Salmon acquired this migratory ability by developing a plethora of physiological adaptations. Not only do their kidneys adapt to being in salt water, but also these fish chemically alter the way in which they see prey and predators depending on whether they're in fresh or salt water.

A CHANGE OF VIEW

Once a salmon, steelhead or coastal trout species migrates to

As a salmonid's visual pigments shift once entering fresh water, cerise is one of the first new colors to stand out. This is a good color selection for returning salmonids.

saline environments, most of their color vision relies on the cone pigment rhodopsin, which is best suited to blue colors around 503nm. The remainder of their retinal color-based prey detection system uses the pigment (porphyropsin) optimally tuned to 527nm (somewhere between blue and green). This is convenient for a pelagic (ocean-going) species because the blue/green environment is mostly what's down there. So it pays to see those colors well.

As the salmonid returns to the tidal or estuarine environment, a myriad of physiological changes occur. Not only is there an onset of sex hormones that stimulates territorial responses, but the visual pigments in their eyes begin a shift to the longer wavelengths, making their vision maximally tuned to "warmer" colors.

We can see the change in habitat color by looking at one of those from space, satellite views of North America. There's a change from the deep blues of the ocean, towards more green and continuing on to a brownish/reddish hue as you approach the coastline. Coastal areas contain organic material, siltation and chlorophyll-containing water, which appear green and brown. These particulates absorb the blue shorter-wavelength colors and reflect only the colors from green up to the redder, longer wavelengths.

Once the migrating adult salmonid returns to the estuary, the retinal pigments shift back to mostly porphyropsin, which suits the freshwater phase (redder or longer wavelength spectrum) of the migration better.

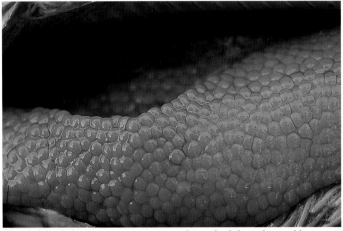

Chock full of pheromones, returning salmon find the color and bouquet of roe as a bait, irresistible. This whole collection of roe is the right ovary. This female's left ovary is seen lying just behind. That dark stripe under the spine is the kidney and the spaghetti-like projections from the female's intestinal tract are termed intestinal cecae. Class dismissed.

From an angling perspective this makes elegant sense and answers an age-old angling conundrum. Why would a salmon eat its own eggs (cured roe etc.)? This is absolutely counterintuitive. Wouldn't the salmonid that eats its own eggs become unable to pass its DNA to its offspring? As a species, wouldn't it die?

I think a couple of things are in play.

First, roe or salmon eggs are the female's ovarian materials. The thin tissue holding a skein of eggs together is anatomically called the mesovarium. The whole collection of roe on one side is considered an ovary. Ovaries (both sides) and their fluids (ovarian fluid) are chock full of hormones, which include pheromones. Pheromones are chemical substances that are attractive to a species. Insects are attracted to insect pheromones and humans are to human pheromones. Fish ovarian fluids are loaded with pheromones that are attractive to fish.

LET'S GET BACK IN THE WATER

Now, you're a steelhead headed upstream, and for the first time you're starting to see colors that you've never seen before (no this isn't the 60's). Couple that with the fact that this strange new color is loaded with "man, this smells good...who is that?" and you've just got to check this clump of strange colored eggs out (remember, you're a steelhead).

You feel rather secure, in a steelhead sort of way, in your yearning to inspect this lump of love because you've developed the good habit that anything that appears contrasting is something to be investigated. So you pick the roe up in your mouth (seeing as how your fins haven't evolved into legs and arms quite yet) and the rest is angling history.

Countershading, or How to Disappear Into Thin Air (Water)

"Lack of awareness of the basic unity of organism and environment is a serious and dangerous hallucination."

Alan Watts

Most fish are dark on top progressively, getting lighter as you go towards their belly. Out of water, this is pretty much the way fish appear.

THE SETUP

Remember that night, walking alone in the bad part of town? Danger, you feared, lurked in the dark. It was late; you regretted dressing so well. Lost and intimidated, you can't stop to ask for directions.

There was trouble a brewin'.

Relate?

This is you, being prey. Repeat that scenario enough and you won't be around very long unless you've got that something special. Special: like a seventh-degree black belt and a pistol.

Danger is everyday life in the food chain. The would-be prey that survives to tell the story does have something special, it's called being invisible...like you wanted to be that night you were walking alone.

LET'S GET INVISIBLE

Getting invisible is easy for aquatic creatures. Some fish disappear by altering their coloration to match their surroundings. A few invertebrates have exoskeletons (outer body structure) that are translucent. Young baitfish are rather clear and some older pelagic (ocean-going) species become relatively invisible by virtue of their silvery sides.

Most sportfish species and their prey become inconspicuous by a mechanism called countershading, an evolutionary adaptation every angler should know about. Incorporate it in your lures to catch fish. If used incorrectly, an improperly shaded imitation will show up as out of place and not as potential prey to a predator.

HOW COUNTERSHADING WORKS: THE DETAILS

We mentioned that as part of the predator/prey relationship, fish developed countershading so they don't contrast with their surroundings. You've noticed that most species are usually dark on the top (dorsum, or dorsal aspect), lighter or silvery on the sides and pale on the ventral (underside or belly) surface. These shading characteristics allow fish to use variations in aquatic lighting to remain unnoticed in a dangerous environment.

TOP DOWN

From above, a fish-eating bird would observe its prey's dark dorsum, blending in with the aquatic bottom. This is due to the

Under water, most of the ambient light comes from above, less from the sides and the least reflects upward from the bottom. Dark color or pigments absorb light. The darker the skin, the more light it absorbs, therefore the less light reflected back to the predator. In other words, the more light, the more pigment you want so you reflect less to the predator. A fish without any pigmentation would appear something like this in water.

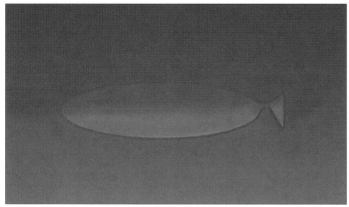

Fortunately fish have pigmentation patterns that reflect light proportionately to their environment. The net result is near invisibility.

REVERSE COUNTERSHADING

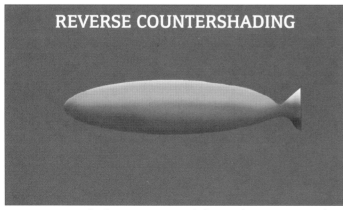

Reverse countershading appears out of place and can sometimes be used to imitate an injured baitfish. Make sure you have a couple of baitfish imitations that are designed to look like this.

bright light penetrating down from above (called downwelling light) onto the fish's back. The dark pigment absorbs most and reflects little of the bright downwelling light. The water's bottom surface reflects light back up towards the fish but it's about 1% as bright as the downwelling light so doesn't light the fish up much in relationship to the downwelling light.

Viewed from above, the dark dorsum of this grayling matches the water bottom almost perfectly.

The overall effect is that a fish viewed from above is about as dark as the aquatic bottom, so the predator can't distinguish an outline. The net result is the fish becomes invisible.

The same fish, if viewed from underneath, sports a light underbelly because it reflects the weak upwelling light. It also blends in with the remaining field of vision, mostly bright downwelling light penetrating from the surface (i.e. light from the sky). Again, the fish appears invisible when viewed from below.

This chum salmon is hard to make out because of its adaptation to environmental sidelight.

The most dramatic effects of countershading come into play when viewed from the side. Convenient for fish, because this is the orientation most predators view their prey.

Suppose for a moment that light intensity in water was all the same (which it isn't). From the lateral aspect (side view), a countershaded fish would look dark on top, light on the bottom and somewhere in-between on the sides.

You say, "No problem, that's how they look to me. . ." Well, fortunately for them, that's not how they look to other fish. Because of countershading, it doesn't matter if the specific color or hue of the fish and its surroundings are the same. What's important is if the shade or bright/dark intensity (luminosity) is appropriate to the light that hits it.

The reason countershading works is because the intensity of fish shading is (inversely) proportional to the underwater light that it reflects. The dark top receives the most light (downwelling), absorbs most of it and reflects only a little. The light underbelly gets only the weak upwelling light, absorbs relatively none so it reflects most of what it receives. The sides get what's called horizontal spacelight, which is about 5% as intense as the downwelling light and reflects it back, proportionately.

The net result, from the side of a fish, is the overall light reflection appears evenly distributed. When the fish matches the environmental light (reflects it back in equal intensity), it appears to disappear.

So if countershaded prey becomes invisible to predators, how do predators discern enough prey to survive?

Well, notice that there isn't any shortage of predators around. So they must be getting around it (countershading) somehow and they're not all just eating insects. . . a lot of predatory sportfish get big by eating vertebrates. One way fish get around countershading is by distinguishing differences in prey luminosity (i.e., contrast in light). And that's what an angler

Dark on top, light underside, a pink salmon viewed from the side, appears to disappear.

should do also: "match the prey" in terms of luminosity.

If the baitfish you're imitating has a dark back, match the degree of shading in your imitation. The same goes with the underside. If the sides are silvery or have scales, chances are they reflect light (e.g., polarized UV and other light) and so should your imitation. A predator's ability to see this kind of reflected light is bad for prey but good for predators (including anglers). Experiment around with your materials (see Chapter 4), try to see the light. . . and then match it.

Chapter Nine

--- ><> ---

Strike Response

"Beware of Romulans bearing gifts."

Cmdr. Leonard McCoy: Star Trek

Pez Gallo (pronounced pes gah-yo"), also known as roosterfish...aggressive on the strike.

I've got to quit spending money on fishing gear.

This time I promise...I'm just looking.

So I tell myself. . . But what if the best place to buy that reel I've always wanted is the Mega-collossal International Intergalactic Angling Expo?

No, I'm just gonna look. . . maybe indulge in a little sport-show cuisine. Steve will be with me, all he ever gets is $15 worth of beef jerky. He'd like to go on one of those exotic angling vacations but says he shouldn't spend the money, blames it on Marney (wife).

I just don't tell mine (Jan). But I'm not getting anything today anyway. Just that coronary-cloggin' corndog and a Diet Pepsi. Oh, if I see a book, that's OK. . . It's educational.

Yep, I got the reel. And you saw it coming.

I couldn't resist it. Blame it on the smell of the hot dogs, the testosterone, bald men in camo, duck calls in the distance. *Not* to buy that reel would have been just plain wrong. I couldn't wimp out, could I? No, as a matter of fact, I was obliged—as a male competing for the top of the food chain. I didn't just buy it, I attacked it, and I got a good deal too.

Furthermore, I'm deeply satisfied at the most primitive level.

THE SCENE OF THE CRIME

There I was, washing down three mustard-slathered corndogs with slugs of Diet Pepsi at the fast-food cafe. Raspily purring like a post-gazelle lion licking its paws, I fondled my new reel with my left hand. Oh, yeah, anglers are animals.

Fishing cohort Murray Wilson tied this successful estuarine stickleback fly. Notice the red ventral coloration. Breeding sticklebacks have red bellies that predators key in.

Male hormones create the hooked jaw and bone jarring strikes. It wasn't until this male got territorial that I was able to get into the fly action.

The differences between the male and female pink salmon are dramatic and due to hormonal influences.

Males are more concerned with territory and are so equipped, females are designed to produce eggs and offspring.

If marketing triggers anglers to spend, it can work on fish to make them bite. A few stimuli combined can often synergize to send a powerful message. It's one thing to resist buying the reel, but put a crowd, the competition, all the smells and the prospects of catching big fish together and I was a goner. That's exactly what those shows are designed to do: stimulate a strike response...from anglers.

BACK TO FISH

You want to know what triggers fish to strike? First, learn what's important to them, then figure out the buttons to push.

Fish need to eat—we know it's important to understand how fish view prey, but what else?

Fish want protection. If intruders arrive on the scene, fish either attack or flee. And there are times when you can capitalize on a fish's hormonal status to get it to attack. You can always make a male fish attack when it's running on testosterone overdrive. A male bass guarding his nest, for example. The same goes for spawning salmon; the males will attack if they're in the latter hormonal stages of their migration.

A lot of fishing lures work by pulling a protection trigger. A quick look through the angling catalog and all you have to do is ask, "Is this imitating something a fish will strike because it's

hungry, or because it's territorial and aggressive?" The lures in the graphic combine visual behavioral triggers. Konrad Lorenz, the father of ethology (animal behavior), knew that his research subjects (target fish) would preferentially strike yellow backgrounds that had a red dot on it. I don't think this phenomenon is limited to target fish, you see it with lots of sport fish. Yellow and black can produce similar results. One of the most time-tested color combinations is the combination of red and white. I suspect it's the most used in angling because of the great contrast it provides (remember target enhancement?).

From a practical perspective, just look in the tackle box of most professional anglers (guides etc.), you'll see a preponderance of red-and-white combinations. From a distance of more than a yard, red, appears gray. As the lure nears the fish, the gray turns to red and I suspect this transformation can stimulate a strike response, particularly when the shift to red occurs on a white background.

Color changes occur in nature, often in hostile situations. Fish can change coloration in response to territorial disputes. They'll "red" up in preparation for a fight. Spotted bass will "flash" their markings before they attack. Lorenz (probably a baitfisherman), did a lot of work with sticklebacks trying to identify common fish behaviors. He found out that a male stickleback's red belly not only attracts the girls, but provokes fights with other red-bellied three-spiners (sticklebacks). That's why, whether fly tiers know it or not, that the little tuft of red works wonders with stickleback patterns and many others.

If I were to make one fly-tying suggestion, it would be this: make the belly region red, not the gills.

Spinning, wobbling, buzzing, flashing colors. . . anything to get fish to come play with us.

Predatory fish know a breeding male stickleback will put on a macho display that culminates in its demise. They've learned that the red coloration on a stickleback translates to easy pickins for the predacious piscine. I also suspect the bright-red Chironomidae (Chironomids) pupae provide a reaction-producing stimulus for lake-cruising trout.

IMITATION VERSUS EXAGGERATION

There's a big difference between imitation and exaggeration. A lot of fly-fishing is about trying to imitate natural prey. But what many fly-fishers aren't aware of is that there's also a place for exaggeration. Flies such as skating bombers and big-eyed flies amplify certain characteristics. So do lots of lures. Many combine vibratory, color, motion, contrast enhancement and predatory components. One reason there are so many different types of lures is that there's a myriad of strike triggers that anglers can use to catch fish.

This was designed by my buddy Larry Heilman. He lives in Alaska and has spent a lot of time on rivers and lakes, both liquid and frozen. This lure has superstimuli, target detection, big eyes and lateral-line stimulation all rolled into one.

Angling tip: Combining triggers. A friend took a successful spinner and combined it with a "hoochie" or squid imitation. Worked great for chinook in fresh water. These guys are used to eating squid in the ocean and might work well for ocean species like tuna also. Don't be afraid to combine things, try new ideas. Take a look at the picture on pg. 70 and see if you can't come up with your own "superstimuli" or color-sensory enhanced combination.

RETRIEVES

Now that we've got our imitation in the water what do we do? Fast retrieves or slow retrieves, which is better for eliciting a strike response?

Well, let's think about this for a moment.

My buddies Dave and Brian like to troll for lake trout in the California foothill lakes. They're speed devotees. Their take on the retrieval speed issue is "if it can't catch a quick lure, it's too small." Granted, this is a narrow perspective, but it makes me look to nature to see if there's a biological precedence for fast retrieves.

Evading prey doesn't dally while escaping from predators. Baitfish boogie when they can, so should your retrieve. This kind of approach seems best when you're fishing in two dimensions. By two dimensions I mean surface fishing. You're not fishing very deep, you're just concentrating on close or far, right or left, water surface regions. Casting and slapping flies and lures close to shore while using very quick retrieves will often stimulate surface-lingering predatory fish to strike. I know, I've done this a lot for big browns at dusk on the Yellowstone.

TAKING IT A LITTLE DEEPER

When you're trying to fish the entire water column, things are different. You're really searching for fish in three dimensions so you have to vary your retrieve. And the type of lure makes a difference. If you're fishing Chironomids, you should go slow, this is how the real midge larvae behaves in lakes. Use fast strips with leech patterns and spoons. Go slower with nymphs and spinners.

Eye See

". . . it seems that it would take less than half a million years to evolve a good camera eye . . . It's no wonder 'the' eye has evolved at least 40 times independently around the animal kingdom. . . It is a geological blink."

Richard Dawkins

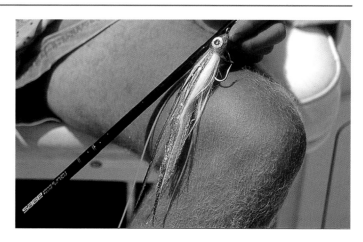

Big-eyed flies say, "Take me, I'm vulnerable."

Colors, shapes and forms create emotional responses. Whether we're aware of it or not, our underlying responses to what we see shape our decisions. What do big eyes mean to you? A good example is those weird velvet paintings. The ones of big-eyed children that scream, "I'm vulnerable."

We're constantly sizing people up. Unconscious decisions are made regarding how to interact with someone based on how they appear to us. Does this person look friendly (upturned mouth, big eyes) or hostile (downturned mouth, angular shaped eyes)? These decisions get made daily whether we're at the corner store or walking down the street.

This might seem unusual but eye morphology conveys specific meaning to many animals.

And herein lies my point.

Big round eyes connote safety. Eyes also often define which

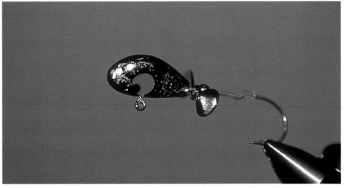

I don't know if a jig with crossed eyes works better than one that's not cross-eyed, but the eyes are prominent.

A well-known pattern, this Deceiver has noticeably big eyes and a good color combination.

A professional saltwater angler's fly box loaded with big-eyed imitations. What if we tied flies that were only eyes, a dark back and the rest was clear? I'm sure there's some out there.

end of the fish bites. Animals have come to rely on eye morphology and placement in day-to-day survival. A common evolutionary deceptive ploy is for fish, or other aquatic creatures, to develop an eye-like marking on their tail.

In normal situations, when a predator approaches, it identifies the front of the prey (which usually leads the escape route), in order to intercept it. Fish that have acquired rear-mounted eye markings are able to "fake out" their predators and escape in the opposite direction to the predator's lead.

For this reason, fish pay attention to eye shape and placement.

WHICH EYES TO USE?

A look at the predator/prey illustration in Chapter 8 is all it takes to know which eye morphology a predator would prefer to attack. Remember that it's an aquatic jungle down there so fish have to constantly stay on guard. Chasing prey with down-turned mouths and angular eyes is risky business. Does this mean you should paint smiley faces on all your lures?. . . well, maybe. Make the mouths small. A big mouth means big bites to a fish. For certain, don't put angular eyes on them and don't make them too big.

The angling tip is, "don't give your intended quarry too many reasons to pass your presentation by." As fishers we're in the sales business, the prey imitation business. We don't want to send the wrong messages.

Superstimuli

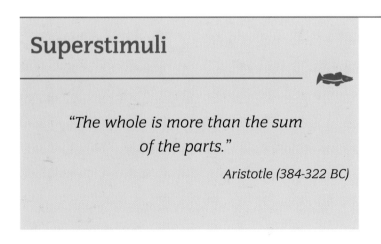

"The whole is more than the sum of the parts."

Aristotle (384-322 BC)

My preferred form of angling—fly-fishing, has a little something for everyone. You can get as involved as you want. Some anglers just want to catch a few fish and that's fine. There's lots of "off the rack" feather-and-fur imitations that can help them do that. Some fly-casters consider dry-fly fishing the *proper* way and

they have lots of company in that viewpoint. No, this section is for truly deranged anglers.

Obsessive Compulsive.

You know who you are.

A few of you write about fishing. Some are what I call guerrilla fishers and others you can tell by looking at them.

Irrespective of the moniker or modus operandi, it's not hard to identify you guys if you know what to look for. One peek at your tacklebox and your non-angling friends will wonder if you're out on a weekend pass.

The bugs in your fly boxes are disgusting. Misshapen heads, stuff that vibrates, weird shapes, pungent odors too. . . mostly flies that resemble used cat toys.

Nature punishes consistency and rewards excellence. To take advantage of resources in a competitive environment you have to innovate, get an edge on the others. You know, got to have a "niche" market, be extraordinary, it just sometimes looks ugly, like your flies.

Sure, all fish key in on certain prey types. And we know

My friend Rick Fox tied this rockfish fly. Red/yellow, yellow/black, red/white, are all well-known, highly contrasting, superstimuli color combinations.

there's been a lot of fine work done on matching the hatch, the correct entomological way to fish and best presentations. This isn't extraordinary.

We've all been searching for the masterpiece of flies, one that drives fish wild.

The Leonardo De Vinci of lures, the juggernaut of jigs. I'm talking about the Superstimuli.

Superstimuli is actually unfair fishing. It jerks the neurological chain of a fish. They just can't help but go nuts for it.

But what are superstimuli? And how can you use them to your angling advantage?

OK, fine, let's consider a few.

Superstimuli often contain specific color combinations. As I said, to see examples of superstimuli, all you have to do is peruse

Easy to notice this Cabo San Jose taxi, but that's the idea.

A few of the joys of a crisp Pacific Northwest morning: sunlight, steelhead and a Mars bar, all high-calorie items. Candy marketers are quite familiar with color combinations that produce human strike responses.

the big tackle catalogs and you'll see more examples of eyes that work: yellow iris's with black pupils. Red central dots will work too, just don't make them too big.

Fly attractors like the Royal Coachman use stimulatory color combinations. It's a fly that's got that little something. A Coachman's got colors and materials that combine to form superstimuli, so do Yellow Butt Skunk steelhead patterns. Highly contrasting colors like red/white, black/white or yellow, dark green/light green all will provide more stimulus to aggressive fish than any one color alone.

Experiment around a little and you'll find combinations that work better than any one trigger alone.

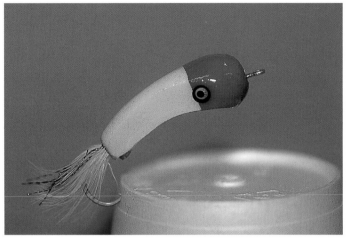

Bass attractor, good wiggling color combo.

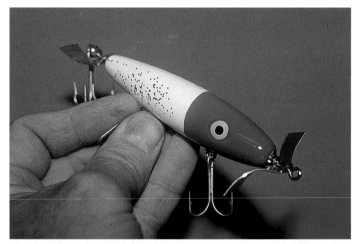

This bass lure, designed decades ago, incorporates near-field lateral-line stimulation (via the propeller, big eyes and color superstimuli). All it needs is a pheromone releaser. . .

Chapter Ten

≈

Field Guide

"The first attempt at generalization seldom succeeds; speculation anticipates experience, for the results of observation accumulate but slowly."

J.J. Berzelius (1830)

Getting ready to go. . . The best insurance against an emergency is being prepared. Cell phones with preprogrammed emergency phone numbers, a whistle connected to nippers and a space blanket are almost a sure bet that you won't need them. (Use a whistle to elicit help when going downstream in water-filled waders). The camera is in case you catch a fish.

Are diaries for sissies? After all, aren't fishing journals really nothing more than angling diaries?

Scientists think the recording of field observations becomes the creation of a field journal and the basis of good science. Great discoveries have been made with the use of a little discipline and the observational record. And the potential value to the scientific angler is enormous.

When we record observations we become aquatic naturalists. Our data becomes a tool to help us become more proficient as anglers. We forget a lot more than we think we do. I suspect there's a myriad of methods and techniques long forgotten not to mention all the beautiful fish and great outings that fail my memory.

FISHING LIKE A LOCAL

We have a tendency to think that the technique that's required to catch a fish is somehow specifically related to the particular geographical area we're fishing. A conversation with my friend Tony illustrates this point.

Tony recalled fishing British Columbia's Gold River last year during the steelhead run. In the course of the conversation, we agreed that the locals were quite adamant about "the way" to fish the anadromous rainbow.

B.C. steelheaders tell you the "proper way" to fish is to use a long (10- to 11-foot) drift rod with a center-pin reel that spins freely. Then as terminal tackle, you string a foam float, followed by a ball-bearing swivel and trail it by evenly spaced, quarter-inch split shot topped off with a small piece of colored-wool egg looped to the hook. Sometimes there's a single Jensen egg or a

glob of roe added to the hook point, but overall, it's a lot of gear to be slinging around your head.

To get to where the steelhead lie, you launch this leaded bolero slightly upstream to get it to the nooks and crannies of the river bottom where the fish lie. I find that I lose a lot of gear fishing this way, then again I'm a beginner at this technique (excuses, excuses...).

Politely, Tony told me how he fished the Gold with a method that's commonplace in Oregon. What he does is take a cork float and suspend a lead-headed marabou jig just a couple of feet below, depending on the depth of the water. Black is a popular color as well as purple and pink. The jigs I've seen used this way produce a good outline by contrasting with the water. This method works well and you don't lose much gear.

"OK, so what's the point" you say?

I used Tony's method about six years ago on the Clackamas and totally forgot it. Out of sight, out of mind.

How many other techniques and secrets remain hidden in my hippocampus (the brain's long-term memory storage facility)? There is been a half-dozen times I could have used that float-and-jig technique but I didn't even think about it. Therein lies the secret. If you write it down, you don't have to remember it. Review your notes periodically and it will refresh your memory not to mention the satisfaction you'll get from recollecting your expeditions.

MY NOTES ARE OKAY, THEREFORE I'M OKAY

Another advantage of compiling field notes is self-esteem. I don't know about you, but I have this tendency to think that I

One of the down sides to photographing this snaky-looking char was that my arm wasn't long enough. Better to slide a fish in the security of the water and take the photo without handling them. Better for fish, better photos.

don't catch many fish. Or better put, I think that I ought to be catching more fish. This especially comes to mind when I look at the money I've spent on gear to support my angling addiction. (I suspect this is either Catholic guilt or some kind of evolutionary programming).

I notice that when I review my notes, I feel better about my angling. Not that the nuns from my grammar school past would approve (I have yet to meet a nun on the water), but it does increase my sense of having gotten value out of the time and resources I've committed to my favorite pastime.

A quick look at my journal tallies my gallery of piscine participants. When you peruse yours, you might find yourself saying, "Wow...that was an eight-fish morning!" That in itself is worth the time spent recording your expeditions.

This fish-slide photo technique is better than squeezing them.

WHAT TO RECORD

This is the best part.

There isn't a one-size-fits-all when it comes to fishing record-keeping. There are angling journals that have pretty pictures or places to jot down aquatic trivia, but not the minutia that makes any difference. Selecting what you want to compile determines the data you'll collect which eventually determines the usefulness of your field journal. You want key scientific information that gets you into fish.

A big issue in science and study design is making sure what gets recorded provides insight to the research questions you (the observational naturalist) are asking. You'll ask research questions like, "Is the time of day or the degree of sunlight, more important to my bass fishing? Does cloud cover make the use of polarizing materials more or less important?" Ultimately, you decide what's important to record not someone else.

The following topics include some, but certainly not all, the potential areas of interest you'll want to consider investigating in your journal.

TIME

Dates, time of day, month, etc. are all critical to include in a fishing record. Fish are all migratory animals whether they live in lakes, oceans or rivers. Migrations are influenced by environmental circumstances. Keeping track of the seasons, lunar cycles and time of day are crucial to your future predictions of catching fish.

"What about barometric pressure?" you ask.

Fish live in the water where the relative barometric pressure is far greater than it is on terra firma. Compound this underwater pressure phenomenon with bodies of water at different elevations and you might see where recording barometric pressure has some merit.

I've seen conflicting reports on how barometric pressure effects fishing activity. Some say it has no influence, but I've found fluctuating pressures slow the fishing and could possibly have more effect on certain species (e.g., freshwater bass versus an estuarine cutthroat).

Record the pressures and see for your self. In the sidebar "Proving What Works" on pg. 80, you can apply a little statistical support for your conclusions.

TIDE AND MOON PHASE

Tides and lunar cycles are important when it comes to brackish (estuary) and saltwater angling. Fish have evolved in the saline environment for millions of years and have learned to use the tides to their benefit.

Develop your knowledge of how fish adapt to fluctuating tides by learning when fish feed in tidal environments. Eventually you can combine knowledge of a given tide and the degree of polarized light penetration. Then I suspect you'll have powerful insights that will produce more fish caught. (You'll see a relationship when the high tide coincides with the crepuscular times of day.)

But then again, you knew that from experience.

TOPICS PERTAINING TO OUR QUARRY

Say cheese...

The human memory is both creative and inconsistent. We sometimes tend to dismiss our recollection of events because we know how imperfect a human memory can be. A well-taken photo is scientific data of the best order and a great memory enhancer.

I usually take my point-and-shoot camera with me when I go fishing. Today's cameras are so sophisticated and automatic that you can get consistently great photos on a routine basis.

Some anglers get a little intimidated with photography. I know this from first-hand experience. It doesn't have to stop us because we all enjoy learning and angling. It's just another thing to add to our angling enhancement arsenal.

PHOTO TIPS

The pocket point-and-shoots are convenient to use and some units are relatively water-resistant, even disposable. Although waterproofing isn't necessary, a zoom is nice and it provides an additional function when you are looking for working fish but haven't brought a pair of binoculars. Just scan the water's surface with your zoom and it will help you spot fish.

If you're going to buy a new camera, I recommend you get one with autofocus. Why, you ask?

I'm forty-eight years old. When humans turn 40, the muscles that stretch and relax the lenses in our eyes lose a little zip and as a result, we need glasses. If you're thirty-something or less and think it won't happen to you, good luck. Anyway, get a camera with autofocus. You'll appreciate it instead of being disappointed at the Wal-Mart photo counter when that big one you released is as fuzzy as the Woolly Worm you caught it on.

FILM

The type of film you use is probably the most important decision. If the photo is for your field notes, a print is good. And you can get duplicate copies to brag with. With a desktop scanner, scan the photo and shrink it and print it as a part of your journal. Try this with Microsoft Excel. Take the saved photo file and insert it into your worksheet then print out the page (check "print gridmarks" in the sheet section of page setup).

If you have aspirations of submitting your photographic record to a periodical, use slide film or 35-mm transparencies. They give much better resolution (clarity) and they're more versatile.

How Fish Work: Angling Journal	Excel Spreadsheet	
Date	*Ruby Lake* March 31, 2001	
Time	4 PM	
Cloud cover	Clear	
Barometric	Rising	
Water temp	47°F	
Ambient temp	?	
Weather trend	Building high	
Lunar Cycle	↓	
Line wt	6 wt. floating	
Rod	4 pc Sage	
Tippet	4' 5x on t. leader	
Weights	no	
Hatch, size, color	#18 Cahill	Caught 8 this evening!
Species	cutthroat	
Size, wt	11'	
Markings	none abnormal	
Gastric contents	N/A	

Home computer made journal pages.

As far as type of film is concerned a couple of things are germane: low-speed (ASA) film has better resolution, which translates to clearer pictures. The downside is they need more sunlight than faster films (higher ASA speeds). For casual use, 400 ASA works fine but if you want to get good-quality resolution I recommend going down to 200 ASA.

BRAND NAMES

Because I don't really know anything about photography, I rely on the experts' opinions. (Incidentally, the way I determine if someone is an expert in photography is I ask them, "Are you an expert?" If he says yes, he's a photographic expert.)

Use my photo recommendations at your own risk. As far as brands are concerned, I pretty much rely on two. I use Kodak for warmer-colored shots (colors above 575 nm) like earth tones, and for vibrant blues and greens (less than 575 nm) I use Fuji.

This Mexican triggerfish photo was taken with Fuji Provia 100 ASA. Lots of blues in Baja.

This photo fits well into thirds, I try to keep the vertical third rule, but the horizontal thirds rule in addition is optional.

COMPOSING PICTURES

My buddy Mark, fish immunologist extraordinaire and master northern pike grappler, taught me to compose a picture into vertical thirds (see diagrams above). Try imagining this in your compositions. Then again, if the fish is going nuts and you're going to release it, shoot the darn shot and get it back in the water. The best photo to take is with the quarry in the water. Shoot the photo with the fish's head just breaking the surface. These can produce great photos and this technique is easy on the fish.

INCLUDING SCALES IN YOUR JOURNAL

On my desk there's a polar bear fang strung on a leather thong that's estimated to be 1000 years old. It's reported to be a shaman's charm found on Savoonga Island. For those of you not familiar with Savoonga, it's near the Chukchi Peninsula, 30 miles from the Siberian Coast where the Bering Strait land-bridge migration was theorized to occur.

Obviously, the bear wasn't the one that got away, nor was it caught and released, but this was apparently a shaman's idea of a trophy mount, just not as conservation friendly as our scale collection.

Believe it or not, you can collect a scale from a fish and then release it much easier that you could extract a canine tooth from a living polar bear. However, I suspect scale collection's a lot more fun (for you and the fish) if you know how. The best way to collect a fish scale is detailed on page 85.

To incorporate fish scales into your field journal, take your scale and mount it in your field guide with a piece of cellophane tape.

That's it, that's all there is to it.

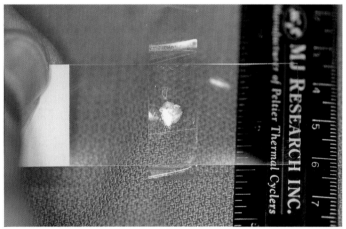

A piece of cellophane tape mounts a scale well whether it's going in your journal, or a microscope slide.

SIZE DOES MATTER

Measuring the length of a fish is common practice. An approximation of a fish's length can be accomplished by placing thin strips of tape on your rod blank at predetermined length intervals. If you want to go to the effort of getting an accurate tape measurement of length go ahead and get a girth measurement too. Here's a formula that allows you to accurately (within a few percent), estimate your released fish's weight with a girth and length measurement.

Fish Weight Formula

$$\text{Weight (lbs.)} = \frac{(\text{girth in inches})^2 \times \text{length in inches}}{800}$$

(divide by 900 for long skinny fish, like mackerel)

A couple of quick measurements and that's all you need to get an idea of your prize's weight...a lot better than winching them up to the gill-hooking variety.

This trout has a parasitic lamprey attached to it. A friend (Bill Drinkwater), who hears everything in the area pertaining to fish, reports a decline next year in the fish population.

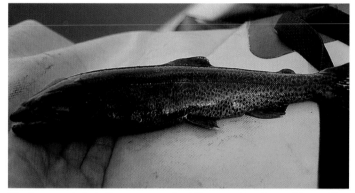

The lamprey infestation compromised the same trout as evidenced by weight loss (gaunt appearance) and melanosis. According to my journal the next year, the lake had a marked decrease in fish numbers. Was this due to the lampreys?

OTHER OBSERVATIONS

For those who have the stomach-pumping predilection, recording a fish's gastric contents can yield important prey information. The same goes for saltwater fish, but getting that information can be somewhat of a rodeo. You might also want to record any pathological information like marine mammal bite wounds or parasitic skin lesions.

The usefulness of this kind of information isn't always apparent until much later. It's quite possible that anglers can provide important disease surveillance information to resource managers (fish and game personnel) when there would be no other way to get the information.

WATER QUALITIES AND GEAR

Temperature, turbidity and flow rates are valuable information. No good field record would be complete without these. Notes on knots, tippets, lures and flies are really important. You can often tell whether you're fishing to leader-wary fish or using the wrong fly by reviewing and interpreting your notes on tippet types and diameter.

PHONE NUMBERS

Aren't cellphones diametrically opposed to what we're trying to accomplish by being outdoors in nature? Not really. A cellphone is a real safety item and it can save lives. You can always turn it off, which is what I do when I'm not using it. If it comes in handy just once for a medical emergency or helps recover someone lost, it's well worth it.

If you're going to have a cellphone, having emergency numbers on hand is a good idea. You can program these numbers into the memory of your phone or you can list a few in your field notes. Include emergency numbers like ambulance, fire, police and a tackle shop in the area you'll be fishing.

I have even used my cellphone while getting skunked fishing. I called Gary at the fly shop, found out what was working and gave it a shot. Kind of digitally matching the hatch.

ANALYZING THE DATA: HOW DO YOU PROVE SOMETHING?

When I first heard about this causality stuff, I thought it was an exercise in the obvious. It's clear when something causes something else, right?

Not really.

Determining causality can be difficult sometimes. And the issue of causality is a concept that I think has created much of the confusion and lack of credibility in the angling arena.

Lack of credibility? Angling?

Yes, it's true; anglers have been known to exaggerate. Believe it or not, I've known anglers to profess, believing it wholeheartedly, that it's the way the brass blade spins, or the presentation or whatever, that makes all the difference in catching fish, when they really don't know for sure. Who's going to prove otherwise?

Could you imagine medicine or agriculture if we didn't know something about the causal effect of things in the world? We would all starve and become diseased, in short order, without an understanding of causality (for those skeptical, remember the bubonic plague).

Yes, granted there's hunger and disease, and farmers do periodically lose crops, but on the whole we are living longer than ever and as a nation we're fattening up like we're corn-fed on the feedlot. So let's bring angling up to speed.

It's time to free anglers from the slavery of causality ignorance, stupidity that has hurt our angling statistics. Our freedom lies in knowing the rules of causality—the 9 rules of evidence. The rules created by Sir Austin Bradford Hill, also known as Hill's Criteria in the science circles.

SIR AUSTIN BRADFORD HILL'S FISH-CATCHING CRITERIA:
The 9 rules of evidence; If Sir Brad were an angler. . .

1. Relative Risk

If Sir Brad was a dry-fly-only angler, he would have loved

This sea louse is a female. The two amber-colored trailing appendages are its ovaries.

this chapter, especially the sidebar on proving what works. This simple arithmetic trick is called the relative risk. Basically Brad said, if your relative risk numerical value is large, you "may" be on to something. (For more on this, see Chapter 10, "Proving what Works.")

2. Consistency

Brad would have liked to "chew the fat" with his angling buddies. He would posit that if other anglers (the credible ones) found that the same thing worked for them in different angling situations and at different times, it would lend support to his findings. In other words, if your other angling friends produce the same results with your method, maybe you're not all wet. But Brad cautions that you can't just stop there, you have to get more evidence to establish true causality.

(Translation: If your buddies agree with you, you're not wasting your time.)

3. Specificity

This is a weak one for angling, I'll admit. Specificity refers to one factor being linked to one effect. This is like saying only one imitation can catch a fish, which we know isn't the case. Sir Brad hedged his bet and judiciously advised us not to overemphasize this one.

4. Temporality

This criterion is often overlooked in our angling detective work. Which came first, the overcast sky or the special spinner blade? Here's another: which came first, the flashy fly or the sunny sky? Not as simple as it seems.

Quite often as we're fishing, conditions change, yet we're still using the same technique or gear setup we were using in a different environmental situation. We tie on a flashy fly, hook a fish, and while we're playing it, the weather changes, like the clouds move in. We admire our catch and say to ourselves "Hmm, cloudy skies...then use flashy flies." In actuality we caught the fish while the sun was out, but we didn't notice that the conditions changed slightly, i.e., like the clouds rolled in. As a result we're inaccurate about the causal relationship.

You can also inappropriately use the temporality concept.

Take the case of the aboriginal tribeswoman. She's pregnant, and while she's on an afternoon walkabout in the outback, a rabbit crosses her path. Quite coincidentally, she goes into labor and gives birth to a baby boy. In an inappropriate use of the temporality criteria, she now "knows" that the rabbit caused her to give birth to this male child and in tribute to the long-eared source of causality, names her child "Flying Rabbit."

What can we say, she had temporality down, but she's missing another criteria for causality, like plausibility (see Criteria # 6).

5. Biological Gradient

This is called the dose-response relationship. This is like using more scent attractant on a lure, and figuring to catch more fish proportionately. Not all causes in nature incorporate biological gradients. For instance, if a little red on a stickleback works, it doesn't necessarily follow that a lot of red will work better. But if a particular element does happen to work this way (like fish hormones or scent attractants), the biological gradient criterion helps build your case for causality.

6. Plausibility

The association of a cause and its effect should be acceptable in light of current biological knowledge or what we know to be true. Don't let the "science is advancing so fast and I can never understand it anyway" conversation, stop you from mentally wrapping around the plausibility criteria. Most science is just common sense.

An example of the plausibility criteria is the case for government spending. A recent survey indicated that more Americans believe UFO's exist than think that congress will pay off the national debt.

Some thing just aren't plausible. We all know the government will never pay off the debt.

7. Coherence

The coherence criterion basically says that your element of causality should fit in with what's known to be true in light of

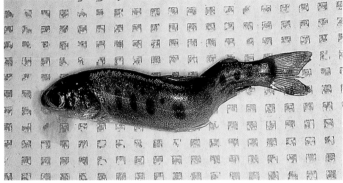

Whirling disease has impacted western America's trout fisheries. Anglers help keep resource managers informed on what's happening in the fish population. Here's an example of a rainbow trout fingerling with Whirling disease. Whirling disease effects a fingerlings cartilaginous spine.

the natural history of your topic. For example, it wouldn't be coherent talking about catching an ocean-dwelling dorado in a backyard pond. It doesn't fit with the natural history of the species, so much so that it's absurd to consider it.

8. Experiment

If you do experiments (as anglers, we can do a form of experimentation called a clinical trial), you might find associations as described in the "Proving What Works" sidebar on page 80. If you were to find association in your angling experiments, it would add considerable weight to your causality argument.

9. Analogy

The case of analogy is best illustrated by yet another analogy. Take the barbless hook topic as a cause for losing more fish. Let's say you've already demonstrated a causal relationship there (e.g. that you'll lose more fish if your hooks are de-barbed) and are now looking at whether a certain knot's predilection to breaking causes you to lose more fish also. You've already established that hook terminal tackle characteristics can lose you more fish, so as an analogy, you investigate whether tippet knot characteristics can be causal in losing fish also.

The Big Picture

None of these criteria are to be taken alone as proof of causality, because causality is an argument that has to be built over time. You can begin to build this argument with the data that you collect in your field journal.

If you make sure that your data and notes are complete, you may find that one day you made a real difference to the sportfish resource. It's the fieldwork and careful observations that become the sentinel of emerging fish epidemics and catastrophes. Problems like these are a lot simpler to handle, early on.

Constructing the Field Journal

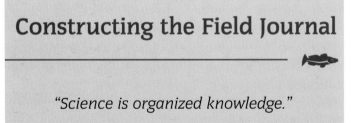

"Science is organized knowledge."

Herbert Spencer (1820-1903), English philosopher

The design of my current field journal is built upon the corpses of half a dozen previous ones. Originally I thought, "No need to get extravagant, just buy a dollar spiral notebook and put it in your pocket." That was a bad idea. I wound up with a 4x6-inch, wire-bound pocket-wad of wet mush. Turns out regular paper gets pretty soggy from humidity, and trying to write on it in the drizzle doesn't work well.

The next cadaver was one of those fancy journals you buy in the fly shop. You know the ones: fantasy, leather-bound jobs, replete with glossy pictures of flaxen-haired young ladies fly-fishing the Madison. I consider these to be great fly-fishing fiction. Ultimately, once I got past the notion that "I'm cool

because fly-fishing is cool," this style of journal was orphaned.

The next mortality was the predecessor to the current version. It had the hard cover I liked and the right texture of paper to write on, but it had a couple of fatal attributes. It was too big and the paper was again too absorbent.

There are two things I like in a notebook: a hard cover to press on and the gratifying tactile purchase of a graphite #2 plastic pencil leaving its mark on the paper. If it doesn't do this, I'm left unfulfilled.

Doggedly, I continued my search for the perfect journal.

I saw one version that got me going. It was a published one that had all the criteria pre-printed so all you had to do was check boxes and fill in the blanks. I liked the attention to detail but there was a problem. It was someone else's idea of what should be written, not mine.

That was it! Each angler has to decide for themselves, what's important and what information doesn't deserve sacrificing rare graphite and trees.

PERFECTION

My ideal journal is waterproof. I like pencil as opposed to pen (you can buy waterproof space pens by Fisher). I found some waterproof spirals at the local outdoor equipment store, but I wanted something more substantial, yet still retain the paper's

The ideal angling log is one that gets used. Keep them small enough to carry around, large enough for record keeping. The water-resistant types work well.

Detailed notes enhance your memories when you read them later. You can get value from your efforts years later. Who knows, they may be the beginnings of your own A River Runs Through It.

water-resistant qualities. The same company (Rite in the Rain) that makes the spiral also makes little binders and waterproof paper fillers for it. After quite a search, I found the right notebook materials and I like the color of the cover too.

The plastic covers of the journal are nice. The paper writes well and it's durable. An advantage of the binder type is that you can archive the pages and add more as you need. I think this is the making of an honest journal.

(I've developed an appreciation for things that prove reliable over the years, like my autowind wristwatch and my dodge pickup. They're both waterproof too. Hmm, I suspect this fondness for consistency is a sign of getting older).

My journal customization includes a few metric conversions, gas mixing ratios, a pocket for incidentals and a checklist for specific data to record. I have the checklist visible which eliminates the need for expensive preprinted forms. The notebook fits nicely in most vest pockets. It'll take abuse too. Originally these notebooks were designed for loggers and sur-

veyors in the Pacific Northwest. I don't intend to work nearly as hard at angling as those guys did at their jobs, so this journal should last me a lifetime.

CHECKLIST

The checklist is arranged so that particular observations are grouped together visually. Line one contains particulars related to time, like date, tide and moon phase (fill in the "O" like it is the moon). The next grouping is the light quality, like cloudy, bright, crepuscular, indirect, shaded or dark. This is related to weather (Wx) which has barometric implications. A low barometric pressure signals the onset of a low-pressure front moving through. Rapidly diminishing pressures can indicate oncoming storms and poor fishing. A constant high (pressure, that is) is often good for fishing.

Looking at the data over a period of time and doing a few relative risk calculations might shed some light on the significance of the barometric readings. You should chart water characteristics like temperature, turbulence and surface (glassy or rippled) condition and match them to the current or flow, which can be often overlooked.

The mandatory fish statistics come next, followed by the results of a stomach pumping if you're inclined towards gastric analysis. Quite possibly the most important parameters are the methodology and instrumentation used to retrieve a fish (gear and flies or lures, etc.). The gear is important, as well as how we used it. There is a big payoff for keeping notes while fishing.

A fish scale that's collected can be folded into one of those sticky backed Post-its and adhered to a page or slipped in the vinyl pocket to be included later after examining it with a hand-magnifying lens. You can paper clip the used pages so your book automatically opens to the current day's entries.

Any forgotten physical characteristics of the fish are irreplaceable later on, so record more of these than you would normally. You'll be happy you did later.

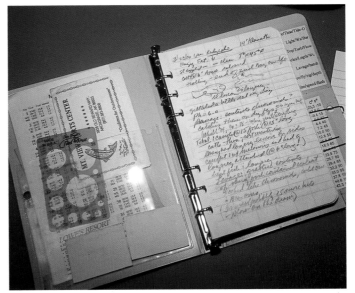

Maximizing information: lists to jog the memory, plastic pockets for cards, rulers, etc. A few of those sticky Post-it notes always come in handy.

Proving What Works

> *"When you can measure what you are speaking about, and express it in numbers, you know something about it; but when you cannot measure it, when you cannot express it in numbers your knowledge is of a meagre and unsatisfactory kind; it may be the beginning of knowledge, but you have scarcely, in your thoughts, advanced to the stage of science."*
>
> *William Thomson, Lord Kelvin (1891)*

What would you say about the following statement? "It doesn't make any difference to me whether a hook is barbed or not, I land just as many fish regardless, so barbless hooks don't make you lose more fish." Personally, if I heard someone say this, I'd think they were goofy. My personal angling experience is that I lose more fish with barbless hooks. But how would I know for sure? How could I prove it?

The nature of proof is a tricky matter all together. I've heard people say, "you can't prove anything." Others believe that all statistics are lies and as a result they become resigned about statistics, and the matter of causality, and go on believing what they want.

So what do most of us wind up believing? Pretty much whatever anyone we think is a better angler than we are tells us.

Unfortunately, this is usually determined by extended bragging matches, where the victor becomes decided by pulling rank, angler-style.

Rank pulling, when used in lieu of gathering evidence, goes something like this (pick one of the following): a) I'm a famous angler, b) I've caught more fish than you, c) I'm an expert/professional fish-guy, d) I'm genetically superior to you or e) I'm packing heat.

Translated this means "What I say is the way it is." If you ask them to prove it, things get a little tense, because most of us don't have any familiarity with proving things.

FISHING CONTINUING EDUCATION

It seems that lately while perusing the angling literature (my monthly fish pornography), I see lots of articles by authors that go something like "my data indicates, or my results show. . .). Easy to say, but in order to apply scientific rigor to the claims, they must be backed by data.

Wouldn't it be a breath of fresh air to include some real data in articles? This way, not only would the author be able to derive first-hand inferences from the data, but so would the readership, anglers like you and I.

WHERE TO START

In the construction of an angling journal it's important to categorize your data. But what kind of data should we keep (see previous, Chapter 10) and how should we set it up? Let's use our barbed vs. barbless catch statistics as an example.

Say I go out for an evening of dry-fly fishing on a nearby lake, which has been recently stocked with hatchery fish. In this example we'll use hatchery fish because they're typically hook-happy and make even anglers like me, look good fishing for them. Say I select a size-18 Parachute Adams. Now if only a few fish are caught, I really can't make much inference from my results because with increasing numbers, comes reliability of cause, but with a little forethought we can set up our clinical trial so we can establish causality.

We've all heard stories about those 30-fish nights, so for this example we'll take advantage of it. We're going to attempt to catch 30 fish and we're going to strive to keep all things equal except for the difference in hook-barb status. First we'll use a barbed hook for a specified period of time and record our results. Now use the same fly, but this time, pinch the barb and see what happens. Once we're complete, we compare our results.

Ultimately what we're doing here is developing risk factors for keeping or losing fish. We've all heard of risk factors. A familiar example of a risk factor is cigarette smoking and its relationship to heart disease (e.g. if you have the factor of being a smoker you run the risk of heart disease).

Hook Status Clinical Trial			
	Lost	Landed	Total
Barbless	11	7	18
Barbed	3	9	12
Total	14	16	30

A clinical trial designed to see if barb status causes the loss of more fish.

In this example, we're looking at whether the barbed status of a hook is a cause of losing fish. The barb is the risk factor and losing or keeping a fish is the outcome we're interested in. The risk of losing a fish with a barbless hook becomes the numerical value of the fraction of those fish hooked and lost on a barbless hook, divided by all fish hooked on a barbless hook whether they were lost or landed.

The math is 11/11+7 (which is 11/18 = **.61**). The 11 goes on top (numerator) because the number of fish lost with a barbless hook was 11 and that's what we're interested in. We used 11+7 as the bottom of the fraction (denominator) because these were the total number of fish that came in contact with our debarbed hook (whether we landed them or not).

Using the same logic, the risk of losing a fish while fishing barbed is 3/3+9= **.25**.

We want to determine the risk of losing a fish while using barbless compared to the risk of losing a fish while fishing barbed (which is .61/ .25). This is called the risk ratio (a.k.a. relative risk) and in this case is .61/.25 = **2.44**

So what does this number mean?

If our risk ratio (final number) were 1 instead of 2.44, it would mean that you'd be just as likely to lose a fish regardless of the barb status, so this would make you think that it doesn't matter whether your hook has a barb or not. If the risk ratio were less than 1, it would mean that barbs were more likely to make you lose fish (we wouldn't expect this). And if the risk ratio is 2 or greater (as we see in this case), it means you're more than twice as likely to lose a fish with a barbless hook. And conveniently, this makes intuitive sense given our experience in nature.

It takes a little practice to set up these scenarios, but once you get the hang of it, your streamside conversations have a little more bite to them.

The next time someone asks you why you're so certain that your new spool of TitaniumX tippet breaks more often than Spongy-spool, you can tell them that in the field trial you conducted as a scientific angler, the Relative Risk of TitaniumX breakage was greater than 2.

Ultimately, doing what works provides for memorable moments such as this. . .
Indian summer afternoons with estuarine caught coho and man's best friend.

Chapter Eleven

━━━━━━━━━━ 🐟 ━━━━━━━━━━

Fish Handling

"If we didn't die, we wouldn't appreciate life as we do."

Jacques-Yves Cousteau

The best way to let life slip through your fingers. . .

If you want to have a little fun, just go down to the local tackle shop and take a little survey on the best way to handle fish. You'll be surprised at the variability of responses. Two things are certain: all the respondents will have an opinion about proper fish handling and few of the answers will be the same.

Okay, I'll grant that I hardly think this is humorous. It's certainly unsettling to me. In fact, some might accuse me of taking this issue way too seriously. But maybe I'm overreacting to something that should be reacted to anyway. I'm convinced that if we don't start taking fish handling seriously, we won't have much reason to go fishing in the future.

Look at what's happening. You can't read a paper or turn on the TV without hearing something dire about the fisheries. Everything is threatened, and so is angling, but it needn't be. Sportsfishers are not the problem with the fishery. We don't catch the numbers of fish that could effect the resource, but we are the most visible.

The best way to be part of the solution is to know a lot about fish. I don't mean angling stories, I mean getting the real facts on fish. How they work, what they do, what effects them and the best way to handle them. Granted, this is a slightly different conversation if you're going to keep and eat the fish. But even then, it would be wise and humane to know the best way to have your quarry meet its maker. (There just can't be enough said for the correct bonking technique.) We need to know the best way to handle a fish that we're going to release, so it will survive and spawn more little sportfish. Either way, we need to be educated stewards of this resource.

Here's the grim reality: A lot of well-intentioned anglers kill fish unknowingly. Post-release fish often die from over-exertion, stress, hypoxia and gill damage, even though the fishers tried their best.

A LINK IN THE FOOD CHAIN

Let's get real for a moment. We all know where those cute little plastic-wrapped trout packages at Safeway come from, so we're not kidding anyone here. Human beings are in the eating business and we're omnivores. Even though most of us aren't subsistence anglers, we all need to maintain our right and access to angling.

As stewards, we need to be on top of this fish-welfare issue, armed with good information and facts. Let's develop opinions based on science and not sentiment. I believe the rational approach will win out.

FISH FOLLIES

Just about any discussion of fish handling advises anglers to protect a fish's mucus coat or slime layer. Anglers read this and then on the next outing streamside, what you see are well-intentioned anglers gingerly grasping slippery fish. But, instantly what's intended as a gentle grasp now results in a piscine projectile launched from hand to terra firma.

Let's say we take a look at what's going on with mucus and fish? Then we can get an idea of the best way to hold a fish.

MUCUS, IT FEELS LIKE IT SOUNDS. . .

Fish produce mucus to provide a general barrier to the environment and as a means to reduce friction for swimming. Mucus production varies among fish species and as a result some fish are harder to handle. Anglers have come up with some innovative ways to overcome this. You'll see all kinds of gloves: Cotton gloves, rubber grippy gloves, fingerless gloves, you name it. Some methods are better than others but remember that dropping a fish to the boat bottom or onto shore is much more damaging than removing some mucus. Too much concern about mucus and not enough knowledge of fish anatomy and physiology is bad for fish.

How hard to hold a fish usually depends on how long they've been played. The longer you play them, the easier they are to hold, though it's never good to play a fish too long.

The current trend towards lighter gear contributes towards fish getting played to lethal exhaustion. It's more fun and it

Years ago, this egg pattern-caught rainbow did a face-plant on the rocks shortly after this photo was taken. I should have kept it over the water. . .

takes a lot longer to land a fish with lighter gear, but you need to stay tuned to how your fish is doing. You want to play a fish quickly, not forever.

HOW LONG IS ENOUGH?

How long do you play a fish? Well, it depends on a few factors. First, consider the water temperature. The warmer the water,

the less the fish can tolerate exertion. We all know from experience that muscular exertion generates a lot of heat. The shivering mechanism is the conversion of muscular cellular energy (ATP) converted to muscle contraction and heat. As previously stated in Chapter 2, fish have narrow temperature operating ranges and it doesn't take a lot of muscular exertion to drive up the core temperature beyond optimal.

Some fish handle exertion better than others. Warmwater species like bass, panfish and carp are much more tolerant to temperature increases than salmonids. During the summer months, you should play salmonid species (salmon, trout, steelhead, grayling, whitefish) quicker than you would warmwater varieties.

HOW LONG DO YOU PLAY A BIG UN?

When we talk about big fish, a lot is left to interpretation. I like to think I catch a lot of big fish, but on average, they're pretty small. Big to me is over 10 pounds. Most of us are catching fish smaller than 20 inches. Small fish can tolerate higher temperatures better than the big ones because they have a higher skin-area-to-weight ratio (more skin radiating heat per pound).

Landing big fish is a rodeo event all in itself. Handling these guys requires a different skill set. You should use handling aids like Midstream's Landing Hand, a good set of pliers to remove hooks and non-traumatic nets. And leave the ultralight rods in the truck.

Finding just the right point of exertion takes some experience so it's better to bring in a fish too quickly than too late. A fish that still has too much energy (a.k.a. green) will be harder to hold and more likely to be dropped. Whatever you do, make sure you hold them over water and close to the surface. A belly flop from high altitudes can cause damage too.

Number 1 safety tip: A green fish can jam a hook in your hand and then decide to launch. Anyone who has removed a deeply embedded hook from his or her hand has an instantaneous spiritual conversion to barbless hooks.

Fish CPR

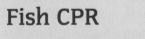

"You will die of suffocation, in the icy cold of space"

*Kang (Day of the Dove),
from Star Trek: The Series*

I said it before and I'll say it again, well-meaning catch-and release-anglers are killing fish every day.

Sounds preposterous doesn't it? Unfortunately it's true.

They're well intentioned, it's just that they don't know a lot about how a fish is constructed and how fish ventilation occurs.

Does it sound odd to hear that a fish ventilates? Well, that's exactly what happens. Fish have to move oxygen past their gills much like we have to move air in and out of our lungs. Fish gills and our lungs, both function as gas-permeable membranes which allow needed oxygen diffusion into the bloodstream.

When the dissolved O_2 in water seeps through the gill membrane, the hemoglobin protein in the fish's blood grabs and carries it to the muscles and organs. This is, of course, what occurs in a perfect fishworld.

What usually happens? You've seen it time and time again. An angler catches a fish, plays it a long time and attempts to release it, but all doesn't go well for the piscine participant. I've had this happen while trying to revive a fish streamside. I was doing nothing more than plunging it up and back, like a semi-comatose, oxygen-depleted pool cue. Eventually the fish came to and made a few muscular tail twitches and took off.

I felt relieved that I didn't do any harm. But I'm not really certain that I didn't do harm. It was just wishful thinking.

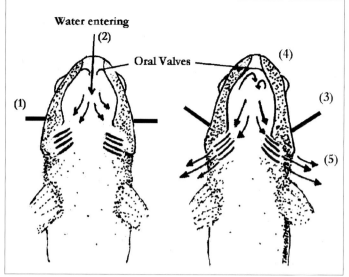

As a trout opens its gill plates (1), the oral region (pharynx) acts like a bellows, sucking oxygenated water past the oral valves (2), as the fish closes its gill plates (3), the water causes the one-way oral valves to close shut (4) as a result, the water can only go past the gill arches which contain tiny, oxygen-extracting gill filaments. The O_2-extracted water exits the fish via the opercula (gill plates)(5).

There's a lot we can do to increase the odds that a fish will do well post-release. Ram ventilation is one of them.

RAM VENTILATION

Ram ventilation sounds like it has something to do with a 1967 Dodge Challenger's intake manifold. The analogy isn't totally unrelated. Ram Ventilation is forcing high flows of oxygen-rich water past a fish's gills. And getting oxygen to a fish's spent muscles and neurological tissue (e.g. brain) via the gills and circulation, is what it's all about.

Sometimes a fish will keep its gill plates and mouth closed during resuscitation. There's no way you can get water to the gills with this situation. Eventually, the fish becomes so oxygen deprived that it seems to lose consciousness. Only when it relaxes and opens its gill plates and mouth does water get in so the fish can get oxygen. The best way to ensure adequate ventilation is to intervene when things aren't going well.

A quick way to revive an overplayed fish is to slip your index finger in the side of its mouth.

NORMAL VENTILATION

Normal fish respiration works a lot like a bellows. You know a fish is ventilating if it's opening and closing its gill plates (opercula). When the opercula open, fresh water is sucked past the lips and into the pharyngeal (throat-like) cavity. As the fish closes its gill plates, an oral valve flaps shut (see diagram) and the pharyngeal water is forced caudally through the gill arches and past the gill plates.

Point the fish upstream and allow the current to fill the mouth.

Once the oral cavity is filled with water, the pressure of the incoming flow opens the opercula (gill plates) and allows fresh oxygen-rich water past the gills.

If the mouth and gill plates are closed shut, water can neither get in nor out. This is where you can use ram ventilation.

DON'T DO THIS WITH A BARRACUDA

If a fish doesn't have sharp teeth, you can slide an index finger alongside the fish's mouth and crack it open a bit. If the water you're fishing has some current, just point the fish headfirst into the current and the water's hydrodynamic force will accomplish the rest.

When water flows into the oral cavity, the gill plates automatically open as the water pressure forces them open. As the new water enters the mouth, the water near the gills exchanges its oxygen across the gill's membranes, for the blood's carbon dioxide and is now exiting via the operculum, CO_2 in hand. It doesn't take long for this gas exchange to occur and eventually the fish has all the reviving it needs. With a few gentle shakes of the tail, the fish will take off on its own and seek refuge in deeper, cooler water.

It didn't take long for this fish to revive. Once it makes convincing muscular efforts to swim away, let it slip from your grasp.

The joy of letting nature free. Release fish close to the surface of the water.

Scale Collection

"Back off man. I'm a scientist."

Dr. Peter Venkman (Bill Murray)
Ghostbusters, *1984 Columbia Pictures*

Can you tell if that steelhead you just caught is a first-return fish?

How would you know for sure? Scale analysis can help a lot and it's not difficult if you know how to do it properly.

When fisheries biologists monitor a population of fish like steelhead or rainbow trout, one method of analysis is scale removal. Done correctly, the fish is none the worse for the experience and it yields important data. Scale analysis allows taxonomic and life history identification of a species, which lends to the body of information we get on our sportfish resource. An informed angler is a good advocate for the sport and I see nothing wrong with scale collection—if it's done correctly.

THE METHOD

The best way to collect a scale is to use a pair of forceps or tweezers and remove only one or two scales. If too many scales are removed, you remove the primary barrier (along with mucus) the fish has to its watery surroundings.

Take a forceps and grab a scale about 3 or 4 rows below the lateral line, about two-thirds of the way back on the fish. Scales can be collected on those particularly nice trophy fish, and along with a photo, make an impressive record. This allows your trophy to spawn more trophlets. It doesn't take much

A salmon scale microscopically viewed under polarized light. This scale shimmers under polarized light. The reddish area (bottom 2/3) is the part of the scale that's embedded in the fish. The top third is the exposed part of the scale, the part we see. A clear demarcation of a group of rings, called an annulus, can be seen when viewing a scale with a hand magnifier (e.g. 3-4 annuli equates to 3-4 years of age).

practice to be able to shoot a photo and clamp a scale with a pair of hemostats while cradling the fish near the surface of the water.

The information that a scale can yield must to be interpreted with caution. To accurately determine a fish's age, a couple of methods have been devised. Scientists will often examine bony organs such as otoliths (see Chapter 3), which are little bones deep in the inner ear area. They cut these otoliths in half and count the rings (a.k.a. the Canadian logging method of determining fish age). This is a terminal (dead fish) procedure so the scale-collection method is used on populations where it's important that the fish be released, like endangered species.

The rings on a scale, called annular rings, indicate the

intervals of rapid growth and non-growth. Rings on a scale form annually when the animal's metabolic machinery is directed away from scale growth for a period of time, such as seen in overwintering. This isn't foolproof because there are times when a fish being stressed or sick causes ring formation also.

Humans can sometimes see an example of "annular rings" or metabolic shutdown with their own fingernails. An illness episode, like a bout with a severe cold or flu, can create a line where the fingernail originates at the base of the nail. As time goes on, and the nail grows, the line just moves up along with the growth of the nail. Fish have a similar reaction with their scales, only the line is an annular ring.

If a fish is severely stressed or ill, it's cellular growth machinery diverts its operations from basic growing, to dealing with the illness. Then once well, it goes back to growing. A scale interprets this interruption of metabolic growth as the passing of another year and so it lays down another annular ring. When the scale is examined, sometimes it's difficult to differentiate the difference between a ring that indicates the passing of a year or such an illness event.

Scales are a great way to document our angling success. It doesn't hurt the fish and a nice fish released can survive to produce thousands of progeny.

Not a bad trade for a scale.

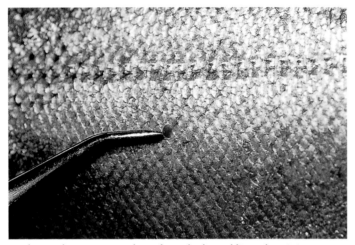

Grab a scale 3 or 4 rows down from the lateral line, place it in your journal with cellophane tape. Instant record.

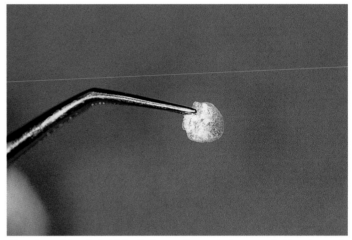

My released trophy's biological record, soon to be recorded in a journal.

More Excellent Fly-Fishing and Tying Books

WHAT FISH SEE
Dr. Colin Kageyama, O.D.

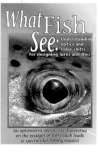

An in-depth examination by Dr. Colin Kageyama of how and what fish see. This important book will help all anglers to design better flies and lures by its explanation of the physical processes of light in water and consequently how colors change and are perceived by fish in varying conditions of depth, turbidity, and light. Excellent illustrations by Vic Erickson and color plates that show startling color changes. This book will change the way you fish! 5 1/2 x 8 1/2 inches, 184 pages.

SB: $19.95   ISBN: 1-57188-140-9

THE FLY TIER'S BENCHSIDE REFERENCE TO TECHNIQUES AND DRESSING STYLES
Ted Leeson and Jim Schollmeyer

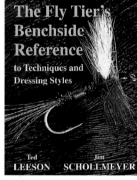

Printed in full color on top-quality paper, this book features over 3,000 color photographs and over 400,000 words describing and showing, step-by-step, hundreds of fly-tying techniques! Leeson and Schollmeyer have collaborated to produce this masterful volume which will be the standard fly-tying reference book for the entire trout-fishing world. Through enormous effort on their part they bring to all who love flies and fly fishing a wonderful compendium of fly-tying knowledge. Every fly tier should have this book in their library! All color, 8 1/2 by 11 inches, 464 pages, over 3,000 color photographs, index, hardbound with dust jacket.

HB: $100.00   ISBN: 1-57188-126-3
CD: $59.95 FOR PC OR MAC   ISBN: 1-57188-259-6

HATCH GUIDE FOR NEW ENGLAND STREAMS
Thomas Ames, Jr.

New England's streams, and the insects and fish that inhabit them, have their own unique qualities that support an amazing diversity of insect species from all of the major orders. This book covers: reading water; presentations for New England streams; tackle; night fishing; and more. Ames discusses the natural and its behaviors and the three best flies to imitate it, including proper size and effective techniques. Tom's color photography of the naturals and their imitations is superb! Full color. 4 x 4 inches, 272 pages; insect and fly plates.

SB: $19.95   ISBN: 1-57188-210-3
HB: $29.95   ISBN: 1-57188-220-0

SIGHT-FISHING FOR STRIPED BASS
Alan Caolo

Long thought to be exclusively a tropical experience, anglers have begun exploring flats-fishing opportunities for striped bass. In this book, Caolo has created the definitive text on this growing sport. Spectacular photography and clear text illustrate such topics as: sight-fishing waters; striped bass behavior; fly patterns; naturals; spotting the fish; presentations and retrieves; angling strategies; tackle equipment; destinations; and more. Sandy Moret says Caolo understands his subject "light years beyond anything I've ever read on the subject . . ." Jeffrey Cardenas calls it "the definitive account," and Nick Curcione says, ". . . must reading . . . well-written, thoroughly researched, and replete with detailed information . . ." 8 1/2 x 11 inches, 100 pages, full-color.

SB: 25.00   ISBN: 1-57188-253-7
HB: $39.95   ISBN: 1-57188-257-X

READING WATER
Darrell Mulch

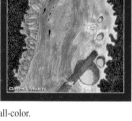

Understanding water currents and how different flies react to them is at the heart of fly fishing. In this very thoughtful book, Darrell Mulch presents his ideas concerning fly types and water dynamics and how you should approach the stream. His drawings are extremely helpful for anglers wanting to know more about recognizing and approaching the different lies fish prefer. 8 1/2 x 11 inches, 64 pages all-color.

SB: $15.00   ISBN: 1-57188-256-1

WATERPROOF FLY FISHER'S GUIDE: WESTERN RIVER HATCHES
Skip Morris
Waterproof/tearproof paper

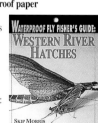

You'll be amazed at the amount of detailed information Skip Morris has packed into this handy-sized book. This waterproof/tearproof booklet helps you identify a hatching insect, select an appropriate fly to match it, and fish that fly effectively. Skip provides useful information, such as: important insect stages; seasons; hatch times; hatch conditions; habitat; imitation size; size of natural, including minimum and maximum sizes; effective fishing strategies; 2 clear photographs of important stages; actual insect size chart; beautiful artwork; fly plates; seasonal hatch chart with major western hatches; and more. This book was written and designed to bring more trout to your flies. 5 x 4 inches, 32 pages.

SB: $9.95   ISBN: 1-57188-230-8

STEELHEAD DREAMS
The Theory, Method, Science and Madness of Great Lakes Steelhead Fly Fishing
Matt Supinski

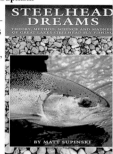

Screaming runs, big, thrashing jumps, relentless power—it's no wonder steelheading is an obsession for so many anglers. In *Steelhead Dreams*, Matt shares all you need to become a better steelhead fly fisherman, including: steelhead biology and habitat; reading and mastering the waters where they thrive; steelhead habits; techniques for all four seasons; effective presentations; tackle; plus best fly styles, casting tips, Great Lakes steelhead fisheries, tying tips, and so much more. If you are addicted to steelhead or look forward to becoming so, you must read this book to learn all you need to know about this wondrous fish and the techniques for catching them. Full color, 8 1/2 x 11 inches, 144 pages.

SB: $29.95   ISBN: 1-57188-219-
HB: $39.95   ISBN: 1-57188-258-

CURTIS CREEK MANIFESTO
Sheridan Anderson

Finest beginner fly-fishing guide due to its simple, straightforward approach. It is laced with outstanding humor provided in its hundreds of illustrations. All the practical information you need to know is presented in an extremely delightful way such as rod, reel, fly line and fly selection, casting, reading water, insect knowledge to determine which fly pattern to use, striking and playing fish, leaders and knot tying, fly tying, rod repairs, an many helpful tips. A great, easy-to-understand book. 8 1/2 x 11 inches, 48 pages.

SB: $7.95   ISBN: 0-936608-06-

HATCH GUIDE FOR WESTERN STREAMS
Jim Schollmeyer

Successful fishing on Western streams requires preparation—you need to know what insects are emerging, when and where, and which patterns best match them. Now, thanks to Jim Schollmeyer, the guessing is over.

Hatch Guide for Western Streams is the third in Jim's successful "Hatch Guide" series. Jim covers all you need for a productive trip on Western streams: water types you'll encounter; successful fishing techniques; identifying the major hatches, providing basic background information about these insects. Information is presented in a simple, clear manner. A full-color photograph of the natural is shown on the left-hand page, complete with its characteristics, habits and habitat; the right-hand page shows three flies to match the natural, including effective fishing techniques. 4 x 5 inches; full-color; 196 pages; fantastic photographs of naturals and flies.

SB: $19.95   ISBN: 1-57188-109-

Ask for these books at your local fly/tackle shop or call toll-free to order:
1-800-541-9498 (8-5 p.s.t.) • www.amatobooks.com
Frank Amato Publications, Inc. • P.O. Box 82112 • Portland, Oregon 97282